An Angel's
Illustrated Journal

It has taken sixty years to explain why
she was on the *Mactan* and not a prisoner

FLORAMUND FELLMETH DIFFORD

ISBN 0-9768272-0-4

Chapters of Life Memory Books
Julie McDonald Zander
www.chaptersoflife.com
1-888-864-6937

Expression
of
Appreciation

To my husband Wallace Jr.
Our children: Paula, Jim (her husband),
Dana and Mark
and to those who said
"then you were a prisoner."
No, I was not a prisoner.
This tells of a life worth living
and theirs too.

Floramund Fellmeth Difford

2006

Introduction

In my life I learned from the British author Rose Tremain that "life is not a rehearsal" and my sister Therese helped me recognize important events by thinking and saying: "This is it."

One of those moments occurred after sailing on the US Grant from the United States to the Philippine Islands, where we arrived after dark. I stood at the railing of the ship anchored in Manila Bay and, not knowing what the future held for me, I watched the headlights of cars moving through the city of Manila and thought: "This is it."

In this history of my life, I tell of the invasion of the Philippines by the Japanese Imperial forces. When General MacArthur left with his staff for Bataan and Corregidor, he declared Manila an open city. Our troops destroyed anything of value to keep it from the enemy.

I had been asked to volunteer to serve as chief nurse on a Red Cross hospital ship—the first of World War II—called the Mactan.

On December 28, 1941, the last Army nurse left Manila for service at Bataan or Corregidor. I waited alone in the large nurses' quarters at Sternberg General Hospital for three days and nights while the inter-island steamer was converted into a hospital ship. I carried with me a small card that declared I was not a combatant.

We finally sailed December 31, 1941—the day before the Japanese marched into Manila.

The voyage of the Mactan took twenty-seven days, with stops for refueling and supplies at Makassar Dutch Indies and Darwin, Townsville and Brisbane, Australia. We finally debarked in Sydney.

We survived rough seas and a fire in the boiler room. We lost three men: one during surgery, another from critical wounds and a third who jumped overboard.

Whenever people learn that I served in the Philippines at the onset of World War II, I always hear: "Oh, then you were a prisoner. "Well, no, I wasn't." For more than half a century, I have been left to explain how, out of eighty-nine nurses, I managed to escape capture.

Linda Ellis penned a beautiful poem in 1998 called The Dash, which describes how people fill the "dash" between their date of birth and date of death. What follows is the story of what lies between my dashes—the life of Floramund Anna Fellmeth Difford.

Table of contents

Chapter 1: What's in a Name?

Floramund Anna Fellmeth Arrives

Chapter 2: Fort Francis E. Warren

Learning to Love the Military Life

Chapter 3: Setting Sail for Adventure

Traveling Aboard the US Grant

Chapter 4: Fort Mills on Corregidor

Nursing, Acting and Socializing

Chapter 5: War Descends on Paradise

Dodging Bombs and Treating Wounded

Chapter 6: Sailing Aboard the Mactan

Stormy Seas, Death and Uncertainty

Chapter 7: Americans in Australia
Establishing US Army Medical Services

Chapter 8: Life Back in the States
Marriage, Recruiting, Children and Reunions

Bibliography and Appendixes

An Angel's Illustrated Journal

*The Memoirs
of
Floramund Anna
Fellmeth Difford*

Chapter One

What's in a Name?

Floramund Anna
Fellmeth arrives

A baby named Floramund

MY MOTHER CRIED the day the family carried me to church to be baptized. They still had not selected a name for me. I was the youngest of thirteen children. At the time, this was the norm. Two sisters had died before my birth on Sunday, Aug 7, 1913. Only four were boys.

It seems every adult in my family participated in selecting my name. When they returned from church, Mother learned I had been baptized Floramund Anna Fellmeth. They selected Floramund to honor a nun they liked, and my godmother added her name, Anna.

I was born at home in a large sixteen-room two-story brick house on 52nd and Justine streets in west Chicago. My mother had a store built in the front, replacing the garden. She was very enterprising. While Dad worked as an interior decorator, she sold paints. Then she changed it to a grocery store. She even rented the store to the local election board.

My mother enjoyed saying: "We did not make a lot of money, but we fed ours and other families."

My parents, Henry Aloysius and Gertrude Bertha (Stenzel) Fellmeth, were natives of Germany. An uncle of Dad's did well in the States and he sponsored Dad, a talented man who established an interior decorating and painting company. Thus everyone had a livelihood.

Dad's father in Germany, Michael, had been the head forester and a friend of the emperor. Mother's father, Carl, was a metallurgist whose knowledge was at a premium, so he worked in Poland two years and in Russia, moving his wife and daughter with him each time. When he decided to move to the United States, my grandmother informed him it would be the last move.

Mother and Dad met in Chicago and married. We had a very happy home life and stayed active in community organizations and clubs, as well as activities at St. Augustine's Catholic Church.

I recall a very happy childhood. Despite the Depression, I

Henry Aloysius Fellmeth holds me, the baby of his family, Floramund Anna, in Chicago about 1915. Below, I am seen as a toddler leaning against my mother, who is pictured with my older sister, Gertrude, who later entered a convent and became Sister Patricia.

I am seen at the right with a ribbon in my hair at Sherman Park with Duke, Bernard and Monica.

never noticed anything lacking in our home. As the baby of a close-knit family I remained blissfully unaware of the "times."

I did not grow up as a lonely child, but almost as a twin.

My sister Kate, who was five months' pregnant when her husband Henry Winkler died, moved back into our home with her son, Henry "Duke," and later gave birth to a daughter, Monica. They lived with us from the time I was eighteen months old until I reached the age of fifteen years, when Kate remarried and moved out with her two children.

At the same time, a family with two girls—Louise and Amelia Sachs—moved into a family-style bar that faced a street back of us. We became inseparable. Louise became my roommate in nurses' training.

What I call 'knowings'

ALTHOUGH UNCERTAINTY CAN BE a constant in life, I tended to know about things ahead of time. People might call it premonitions. I prefer the term "knowings." I've been blessed with a quiet sense of "knowing" when something important would happen before it actually came to pass. Although I may seem gregarious to others, I tend to keep quiet about my sense of "knowings."

The first time I sensed this special gift occurred in second grade at St. Augustine's Catholic School in Chicago. I had recently made my first communion, wearing a lovely white dress Mother had sewn. While I was sitting in my all-girls class, instruction halted at a knock on our classroom door. In walked Sister Superior and without any prompting the entire class stood. Our teacher signaled us to sit again. The two nuns conferred and then told us to leave our desks and stand in a line against the wall. No one knew why we were standing there, but somehow I knew I had to stand tall. I slowly stretched on my tiptoes, standing as tall as possible. Sister then asked those she indicated to go to the front of the classroom. She had selected four students—the tallest students—to join in the Corpus Christi festival. As the shortest of the four selected, I carried the cross of greens in the following Sunday's Corpus Christi procession in church. If I had not stretched tall, I never would have had this honor.

My second knowing came in the sixth grade while I attended a public school football championship at Chicago's Soldier Field with my sister Therese and her fiancé. During the championship game, I looked across the field and, for the first time in my life, I saw a nurse's uniform. Three nurses, on duty at a medical first-aid tent, wore white uniforms and caps with redlined navy capes. I had never set foot in a hospital. I'd never had a family member in the hospital, either. My mother was the healer of all ailments in our family. But I turned to Therese and said: "I'm going to be a nurse." From that time on you might say I had tunnel vision—one focus and one goal.

My sister Therese

AFTER KATE MOVED when I was fifteen, my sister Therese—who was eighteen years my senior—took an interest in me, the baby of the family.

Every evening, she spent hours talking with me in her room, informing me about life and preparing me for the future. She taught me some wise philosophy I recalled throughout my life, including the important statement: "This is it." She said people must realize the importance of events in life.

Therese worked at an automobile company's sales office. She didn't oppose my selection of nursing as a career or attempt to change my mind. But she did want to expose me to other occupations. She arranged for me to file papers and keep books in her office. She sent me downtown alone to shop for personal items.

She came to the realization that I definitely had my heart and mind set to be a nurse. She then joined me in my efforts. What did it take to be a nurse? She went so far as to interview a nurse.

Therese always told me, "It's important in life to have done things, rather than just talk about them. Do it!"

Several moves and several schools

WHEN I WAS IN SEVENTH GRADE, we moved south to a newer house at 77th and Marshfield with eight girls nearby in my age bracket. Later my parents moved to 77th and Ada Street before returning to the old family home on 52nd Street, which was torn down in 1995.

After graduating from eighth grade at St. Augustine's in 1927, I rode the streetcar every day to high school at Mercy Academy, which was run by very Irish nuns with such thick brogues I felt like a foreigner at the school. At the start of my third year, I asked my parents to allow me to change to Calumet High School, a public school, where I graduated in 1931.

I treasure my pleasant childhood that included trips to Highland, Riverview and Lincoln parks; a boat ride from Municipal Pier to Jackson Park; picnics; visits to the zoo; and, when I was in high school, delivering Christmas baskets to the poor.

Therese, seen above, took me (peeking out the window at her) under her wing after Kate and her children left the home. Therese, who was 18 years older than me, spent hours talking with me in the evenings. At left, I am seen on my first day of school walking with Duke while my grandmother watches from the doorway.

Wanting to be a nurse

WHEN I REACHED AGE EIGHTEEN, I needed to select a training school. Although most of the family supported my career choice, my father didn't consider nursing a proper position for a "lady." I do not recall any other family gathering to make a decision about a family member, but this time my brother, all my sisters and my mother held a family conference with my dad. One of my sisters suggested I go visit friends two doors away. Before I left them all sitting around a kitchen table, I made the statement that if Dad thought I should not study to be a nurse I would not do it. I was instructed to go. When I returned, the decision was made. They had convinced Dad that nursing had become a noble profession. I was free to plan on training; now I needed to decide where to study nursing.

My sister Gertrude, who was now Sister Patricia of the Poor Handmaids of Jesus Christ in Donaldson, Indiana, came home with the information that her order had a hospital near the northwest side of Chicago, St. Elizabeth's, which was attached to Loyola University. She also said the hospital was building a new addition.

My friend, Louise Sachs, had decided she also wanted to study to be a nurse. So, Louise, Mrs. Sachs, Mother and I went via streetcar with Sister Patricia to look at St. Elizabeth's. At the hospital, we received royal treatment. By the time we completed our tour with Mother Superior and the principal of the nursing students, both Louise and I had signed up and received a date for entry as student nurses.

Therese made the decision that I would enter training in all new clothes. She checked with a nurse in an office in her building. We spent days on shopping trips. Then Therese invited the family for the viewing. She laid sheets on the living room floor and displayed everything. She then said to me, "If you never have a trousseau, you will have had one." (As an interesting side note, I married in my military uniform and had left all my clothes in the Philippines, so I didn't have a new trousseau, but I had one at eighteen.)

The Goal

Just to
   reach out
    and touch
     each bit
      of life—

At
   least
     once ...

A poem by Wynona Bice-Stephens from her book, *The Art of Nursing*

I made my First Communion at St. Augustine's Catholic Church in Chicago along with my nephew, Henry, or "Duke." I grew up in the same home with Duke and Monica, the children of my sister, Kate, a young widow. One day at school, I knew I needed to stand tall when Sister Superior came into the classroom, and because I did, I carried the cross in the Corpus Christi procession at church. Below are the other three girls selected.

At St. Elizabeth's, I shared a room with Louise for three years while working at the hospital and learning the skills I needed to tend the sick and injured. During training, I also completed liberal arts classes at Loyola University equivalent to eighteen months of study.

My sister Therese and her fiancé, John, who worked in the same company, visited us every Saturday, bringing hamburgers and other treats. All the nursing students eagerly awaited her visits. We'd have to sneak out of the hospital using the fire escape to pick up the food and beverages she brought.

Nothing could have prepared me for the sudden death of my beloved sister, Therese, who died at thirty-five of a

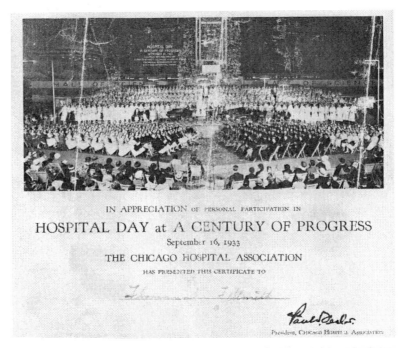

IN APPRECIATION of personal participation in

HOSPITAL DAY at A CENTURY OF PROGRESS

September 16, 1933

THE CHICAGO HOSPITAL ASSOCIATION

HAS PRESENTED THIS CERTIFICATE TO

President, Chicago Hospital Association

Along with other student nurses at St. Elizabeth's Hospital, I sang Land of Hope and Glory *at a Hospital Day celebration in 1933.*

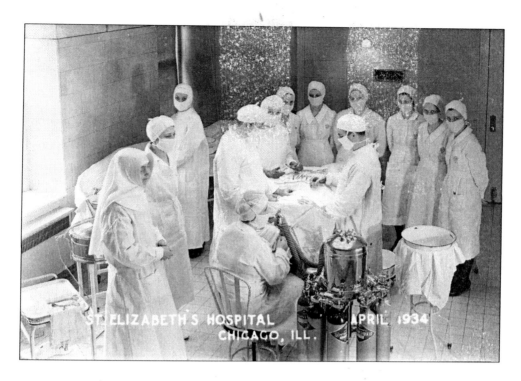

*I am seen looking up,
standing next to
the main doctor
on the left side of the patient
during surgery at
St. Elizabeth's Hospital
in April 1934.
While at St. Elizabeth's,
I decided I wanted to
study surgery and join
the military. I am seen
at left with my friend,
Louise Sachs,
at graduation.*

coronary thrombosis, or heart attack, just two weeks before my capping as a nurse in November 1934.

After the funeral I had to go back to training. I knew I must go on. Therese helped shape the person I had become. She would have insisted I keep striving toward my goals.

The day after I graduated from the three-year nurses' training program, Mother required an operation, so I didn't have much time to mourn for Therese.

An influential movie

WHILE IN NURSES' TRAINING, I went to the movies and saw a film about World War I in Germany. My brother Henry served in that war.

But at the movie, when I saw women in uniforms in an open vehicle at the battlefront, again I experienced that sense of "knowing." That's what I would do. I would wear the uniform of a military nurse.

I didn't talk of my plans to anyone and without saying anything, I started to research how to join the military after nurses training. I wrote to the Veterans Administration and Army and Navy surgeons in Washington, D.C. At that time, the Army planned to increase its nursing corps from 750 to 920. I discovered one of St. Elizabeth's earlier graduates had served with the Red Cross nurses in World War I.

One evening I went to the room of the head surgical nurse. A nurse anesthetist and a floor supervisor happened to be visiting. Believe it or not, I was in awe of them. I didn't mention my military ambitions, but I asked for advice on which hospitals I should apply to for a postgraduate program in surgery. They recommended several.

Thinking it over, I wrote to all of them. It became quite a frenzy at mail time. The nurses wanted me to hurry and open my mail. All of the hospitals accepted me, even though I'd been a middle-of-the-road student averaging about 85 percent because I enjoyed social events and fam-

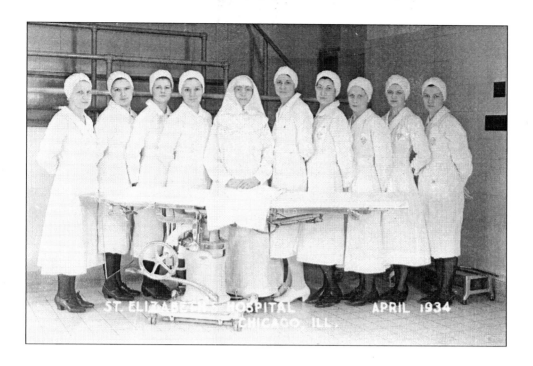

Above, I am standing next to the Sister Superior on the left in this photo of the April 1934 graduating class from St. Elizabeth's Hospital. At left, my friend Louise (right) and I stand beside Sister Patricia (my sister), while my parents are seated before us on graduation day.

On October 24, 1935, I stood at the railing at Bellevue hospital in New York where George Washington took his oath of office with his hand on this railing. On the back of the photo, I wrote: "Someday they will say Floramund Fellmeth stood there with her hand on the railing, not George Washington. (Oh yeah!)"

ily life, too. I didn't spend all my time studying—that is, until I went to Bellevue.

I selected Bellevue because our medical history textbooks repeatedly noted that the first surgeries in the United States took place at Bellevue. In fact, while there, I was the first nurse assistant for the third operation performed on a lung. The gallery was filled with at least 400 students as well as many surgeons.

Bellevue's operating room

To EARN MONEY for the round-trip bus fare to New York, I went on night duty at St. Elizabeth's. During nurses' training, I received $5 a month. My family never had to give me any money, because it cost just pennies to ride the streetcar.

After graduating, I worked as a night nurse in the front office and earned $45 a month. I worked at the hospital for about six months before leaving for New York.

When we arrived at Bellevue, we gave the dean our return trip fare. My family sent me $10 a month for expenses. They didn't seem to be overly concerned about my adventures.

While at Bellevue for six months of specialized training in surgery, I continued to write to the military about openings in the nursing corps.

I remember standing on a balcony along the back wall of the hospital with my hand on the railing. After someone took my picture there, I sent it home with a note on the back that said: "Do you recognize this staircase? Someday they will say Floramund Fellmeth stood there with her hand on the railing, not George Washington. (Oh yeah!) Bellevue, New York, 10-4-35, where George Washington took his oath of office with his hand on this railing."

Without knowing it, I came out at the top of a class of thirty-four when I graduated in 1935. During the exit interview, administrators offered me three supervisory positions as head of a division, such as at Columbia, Cornell or other schools.

I remember the very dignified chief nurse handed me my papers and, for the first time in my life, I'd received A-plus. I had always been a middle-of-the-road student. But in surgery, I excelled.

At any rate, by that time I knew I wanted to join the service.

Both the Army and Navy sent me applications, so I weighed my options. The Army offered more overseas

In this 1935 photo, taken on a yacht, I am seen at right with my friend and fellow student Pat Dolan. Bellevue hospital is in the background. Below is our Bellevue graduating class photo. I am seen second from the left.

options than the Navy, so I selected the Army Nurse Corps.

How I came to be known as Ann

ALTHOUGH I'D BEEN FLORAMUND my entire life—and I still think of myself as Floramund—people in the service called me Miss Fellmeth or Ann.

When I wanted to join the service, Mother went to City Hall for a copy of my birth certificate, which I needed to send with my application. But the certificate stated only Anna Fellmeth. It didn't say Floramund Anna Fellmeth, which is the name my family had given to me. My mother had to vouch for me, stating I was Floramund Anna Fellmeth so the records were changed.

But when I left for my first assignment, I carried with me only a copy of the original birth certificate. On the first payday, the quartermaster didn't want to refuse to pay me simply because the corrected birth certificate hadn't arrive yet, so the paycheck was made out to Anna Fellmeth. So that's how Anna started.

I immediately tried to stop it, but when I arrived in the Philippines and the ship pulled to shore, I saw the quartermaster of finance, who called out: "Ann. Ann. Ann." There it was. I had to keep the name.

While on duty, no one addressed us by our rank, although we entered the service as a second lieutenant. Instead they addressed us all as "Miss" or me as "Miss Fellmeth."

Awaiting orders

MOTHER UNDERSTOOD MY ANXIETY as I waited for orders. Finally, one day I arrived home from work and Mother offered me a shy smile as she nodded toward the cut crystal bowl on our dining room table, where I saw an official-looking letter. I tore it open and read that I would be stationed at Fort Francis E. Warren in Cheyenne, Wyoming.

Army of the United States of America

With the approval of the Secretary of War

FLORAMUND A. FELMETH

of ____ CHICAGO, ILLINOIS ____ is hereby appointed

____ NURSE ____, Army Nurse Corps, with the relative rank of

____ 2ND LIEUTENANT ____, in conformity with Section 10, the National

Defense Act, as amended June 4, 1920 (41 Stat. 767), and will enter upon her duties on

____ August 19, 1936 ____, after taking the oath prescribed by Section 1757 of the

Revised Statutes of the United States.

Oath of office executed
August 19, 1936
Filed in S. G. O.

Form 173
W. D., S. G. O.
(Revised Feb. 20, 1920)
OFFICIAL COPY

/s/ James C. Magee,
Major General, U. S. Army,
The Surgeon General.
Kathleen B. Atto, 1st Lt, ANC,
Acting Supt.

*I waited anxiously to hear from the Army
regarding my orders as a second lieutenant in
the Army Nurse Corps. I was assigned
to serve at Fort Warren in Wyoming
near Cheyenne.*

When I left for Cheyenne, I believe all of my family came to the railroad station to see me off. The great adventure had started.

Chapter Two

Fort Francis E. Warren

Learning to Love the Military Life

I arrived at Fort Francis E. Warren on August 20, 1936. I lived and worked there for three-and-a-half years before leaving for duty overseas.

Entering the Army

BEFORE GRADUATING FROM BELLEVUE in 1934, I sought a nursing position in the Army because I wanted to travel to China.

The life of my brother-in-law, who was a Franciscan missionary in China, fascinated me, so when I looked at the applications, I noticed the Navy offered only Guantanamo in Cuba and the Philippines as opportunities for overseas duty, while the Army provided many more options, including a chance to work in China.

The Navy also didn't operate hospital ships at the time, but the Army did. I didn't know whether it would be better to serve in one branch of the service or another. I applied only to the Army.

Although Mother felt happy for me when my orders arrived, she stood back trying not to cry. Of course, everyone returned home for my going-away parties. My father refused to go to the train station to say goodbye because he was convinced he wouldn't be alive by the time I returned home. I went through that many times with him!

After undergoing a physical and signing papers, I received my official appointment to the Army Nurse Corps August 19, 1936. Many people stood waving farewell as the train left the Chicago station, bearing me to adventures I could only imagine.

Fort Francis E. Warren

I ARRIVED IN CHEYENNE August 20, 1936, having taken the oath of office as Second Lieutenant Floramund A. Fellmeth the previous day in Chicago.

When I stepped off the train, I found a sergeant leaning against a wall. I approached him and asked: "Are you meeting someone?" He replied: "Yes, I am."

The sergeant had driven to the train station in an ambulance and, after picking up my luggage, he drove in silence to the base at Fort Warren and dropped me off at the nurses' quarters.

I met chief nurse Miss Alice Becklin, who had served in World War I. Although she maintained formality, she seemed quite friendly.

She took me to my room, where I met my roommate, Helen Littlepage Locke, a Southern girl nicknamed "Page." The accommodations featured a small living room with a fireplace.

At dinner I met the other six nurses; one remained on duty. Most of us had just been assigned to Fort Warren, since the corps had recently expanded.

Initially, Miss Becklin assigned me to a medical ward, until the surgical nurse went on night duty. The surgeon, Captain Leonard Heaton, later went on to become a major general and chief of the medical corps.

I found life at Fort Warren a tremendous experience. I adjusted well to military life because I am a person of order. So following orders proved easy for me. Most of all I learned discipline. I enjoyed the uncomplicated way of life, working hard while on duty and enjoying my free time off duty.

"Nursing"

A blessed art
of gentle
touch
when
each life
is treasured
much…
kindness
and care
and love
within
are given—
yet
received
again…

A poem by Wynona Bice-Stephens from her book, *The Art of Nursing*

Off-duty life and Wally

DURING MY OFF HOURS, I enjoyed the social life, learned to ride a horse and took up figure roller-skating. I also remember helping others to celebrate Christmas. I shopped at the Base Exchange for patients who couldn't do it themselves.

Officers came out of Reserve Officers Training Corps in college and arrived at Fort Warren in the mid- and late 1930s under the provisions of the 1935 Thomason Act.

One time, my roommate and I had been horseback riding and I had fallen from my horse. We went to the officers' club afterward to have a cold drink.

As we walked to the officers' club for Cokes, we passed a captain—a doctor we knew—who was fencing with someone. Both wore fencing masks.

"I want you to meet, Page—Lieutenant Locke—and Lieutenant Fellmeth," the captain told his companion, whom he introduced as Lieutenant Difford—Wallace E. Difford Jr.

Wally never even bothered to remove his fencing mask. He simply said, "How do you do?"

I bought my clothes from a little department store downtown. One day a saleslady invited a group of us to come for supper and play cards at her home. Wally was there, playing cards. I sat on an old stool listening to radio reports of the flooding in Louisville because I didn't play cards. I didn't pay any attention to him. Then we ate and returned home.

Later Wally asked me for a date. He said he wanted to take me Saturday night to this nice restaurant. He said: "Oh, they have the most wonderful fish dinner."

"Fish?" I said. "I don't object to Friday and fish, but if I'm going on a date, it better not be for fish." As a Catholic, I ate fish or some type of meatless entrée every Friday of my life.

So we want to Romano's restaurant on the south side of

I did duty in a Red Cross tent at the "Frontier Days" Rodeo in Cheyenne, Wyoming.
Below, I started dating Wallace E. Difford Jr. in Cheyenne. Before I left for the Philippines, we agreed to marry when I returned.

I am seen on the left in this photo with Miss Bamsey, another nurse, during Frontier Days at Fort Warren. Below, I sat for nurse Helene Sorenson, who had a new camera, wearing a beautiful dress containing seven yards of satin in the skirt. I left the dress with my mother, who later gave it to a convent for tabernacle covers.

Cheyenne to enjoy a steak dinner.

Everyone saw that Wally kept coming back, but since we had so few nurses and officers' daughters, I still remained in high demand for dances and dinners at officers' homes.

Every time Wally and I would have a date at the movie, I would slip off my shoes because they hurt my feet. But many times the telephone rang during the middle of the movie, and they'd say, "Captain Heaton, you're wanted on the telephone." So, Wally would have to look for my shoes because he knew I'd get called. I think the most surgeries we performed in one month included thirty-four night cases.

My first gardenias

The first time I remember gardenias playing a special role in my life, I had just learned to ride a horse and intended to participate in my first show. Wally said he would buy my boutonniere. But he grew very upset when my flower arrived and I didn't understand why. He explained that the boutonniere should have been a small flower, which was protocol, instead of a large gardenia. I didn't know about protocol with gardenias. All I know is this: I won second place in the horse show wearing that gardenia.

Wally was assigned to Fort Warren for a year. He wanted to fly. But to do so, he needed to remain single. I also planned to do overseas duty.

So we dated and figured we might marry—later.

A long night and a yes

WHEN I WORKED NIGHT DUTY, Wally would stay in the nurses' recreation room and read until I came off duty. One night, after I left work, Wally suggested we go for a ride, even though it was quite late. He had borrowed someone's two-seater car and suggested we drive over the state line dividing Wyoming and Nebraska. At a big wide spot there, cars would turn around and return to the base.

I learned to ride
horseback while living
at Fort Warren in
Wyoming. I am pictured
at right, above, with Miss
Martha Smith in a photo
that appeared in the
newspaper.
At right, I am seen in the
center, wearing
my favorite flower—a
gardenia—after
winning a ribbon
at my first horse show.
I am seen with Miss
Hansen and Miss
Sorenson. We are
wearing the
ribbons we won.

He drove the car and I fell sound asleep. I'd been on duty all day and by two in the morning, I just fell asleep. He stopped at the turnaround and said: "Are you awake?"

I said, "Well, yes, I'm awake."

He said, "I know you have to be married by a priest and I know the children have to be Catholic—" He said, "Would you marry me?" (Wally was Episcopalian.)

I said "Well, yes, sometime," and I went sound asleep.

The next day we had a date.

Wally said, "Do you remember last night?"

"Yes," I responded. "You asked me to marry you and I said someday."

When Wally asked me to marry him, I said yes because I guess I felt that's what I was going to do, eventually. I did not think about marrying at that time. I was on my way to the Philippines. It never entered my mind that I wouldn't go.

When I went overseas, Wally stayed behind to teach fighter pilots.

Seeking Philippine Islands duty

WE HAD TO SERVE at least two years before we could request overseas duty. During the third year, when the time arrived to choose, four of my friends requested duty in Hawaii. I was the only one who selected the Philippine Islands.

My friends tried to convince me to join them in Hawaii. All five pleaded: "Oh, Floramund, come with us. Come with us."

But before I could think of changing my mind, Miss Becklin, our chief nurse, said to me: "Miss Fellmeth. Come into my office, please."

"Do not transfer with friends," she said. "When you become a chief nurse—"

In the photo above, I am seen at the far left in the black skirt and white blouse, photographed with other nurses and First Lieutenant Alice Becklin. At left, I am photographed while relaxing in Cheyenne. Below, I am seen on the right with Bob Crosby and fellow nurse Nona Berman.

Well, it had never entered my mind that I would become a chief nurse. The Army Nurse Corps had only one major, five captains of general hospitals and the chief nurses—the head nurse on the base, a first lieutenant. Your salary increased as your time in the service did, going from $70 a month to $90 a month. A promotion from second lieutenant to first lieutenant also would raise your pay.

Miss Becklin continued: "When you become a chief nurse, two things will happen. When you need to promote a nurse, if you select a friend and she is capable it will be considered favoritism and you'll lose a unit. If your friend is not capable and in honesty you do not promote her, you lose your friend.

"Do not be influenced to change your selection," she continued. "Go to the Philippine Islands."

So I requested duty in the Philippines because I wanted to visit China in the springtime.

When I received my orders for the Philippines, I was issued a list of advisable wearing apparel adequate for tropical use. On the list I saw "lightweight night wear." In my thoughts, nightgowns could be either practical or attractive, but seldom both. The only selection I found was knit rayon. With use of a catalog, I ordered two gowns that appeared attractive as well as practical—one pink and the other blue. With misgivings, I packed them among my other things in a new footlocker, then boarded a train for Chicago, where I spent my leave with my family before traveling overseas.

One of the Cheyenne nurses, whom I met again later in life, said she always knew I'd become a chief nurse. "You didn't know you were going to become a chief nurse?" she asked. I responded, "Well, no, how would I know it?" She said, "Well, everyone else knew."

Before I left, the Fort Warren newspaper ran an article about my new overseas assignment, describing me as "a popular member of the younger social set at Fort Warren." It also stated I would visit my family in Chicago before touring Canada and the Pacific Northwest with my "fiancé, Wallace Difford," and his family.

*Although friends wanted me to
transfer with them to Hawaii,
I requested duty overseas in the
Philippine Islands. Friends at
Fort Warren saw me off when
I boarded a train to Chicago to
see my family before
leaving for overseas duty.
I am second from the left in the
top photo. and at center in the
second photo. At left are my
orders for duty in the
Philippines.*

Chapter Three

Setting Sail for Adventure
Traveling Aboard the US Grant

U.S.A.T. "U.S. GRANT."

I left for the Philippines aboard the U.S. Army transport Ulysses S. Grant, a 508-foot-long steel-hulled ship weighing 15,010 tons and capable of carrying 1,244 troops. First Lieutenant Alice Becklin from Fort Warren, seen with a suitcase in the center of the photo below, saw me off in San Francisco, giving me a large can of popcorn to ward off seasickness just before we sailed April 27, 1940.

Sailing aboard the US Grant

THE OTHER NURSES LEFT FOR HAWAII, and I left Fort Francis E. Warren on March 4, with orders to report to San Francisco April 27 to sail on the Army transport US Grant to the Philippine Islands.

I went home to Chicago on fifty days' leave before traveling to San Francisco April 27, 1940. The steel-hulled 15,010-ton ship, over 500 feet long, could carry more than 1,200 passengers—enlisted men, officers, officers' families and nurses—in addition to supplies.

My chief nurse, Miss Alice Becklin, who had retired from Fort Warren, met me at the dock with a big can of popcorn. Many people suffered seasickness going past the Golden Gate Bridge and it was most severe about five days into the three-week trip, so everyone ate popcorn to settle the stomach and ward off nausea. Most people on the dock saying farewell to family and friends gave them cans of popcorn decorated with ribbons. I saw many such boxes carried aboard.

I felt excited to be leaving for the Philippines; I would be that much closer to China.

As I packed for the Philippines, I brought a long black skirt of beautiful material and sixteen evening tops—all kinds and all colors. What a way to go!

I knew we would have five nurses sailing, so I figured I would share a stateroom. But when I entered my assigned room, I found it filled with boxes of flowers—all addressed to me. Friends and family members sent six gardenia corsages and I received a bouquet of roses from Dad Difford, Wally's father. I didn't see any other luggage. I was the only person assigned to the stateroom.

After we left San Francisco, I went in search of the other five nurses. I found the man in charge of C deck. I asked him about the other five nurses and he said they were in the larger stateroom next to mine.

I went to their cabin, knocked and walked in. Standing in the doorway, I announced distinctly: "I happen to be Floramund Fellmeth."

Minnie Breese told me years later she would never forget that moment when I introduced myself to my colleagues. "We all just looked at you," she recalled.

I saw their room filled to overflowing with luggage.

"I have permission—If you want, two of you can come next door since I'm alone in my stateroom.

So Minnie Breese and Ruth Stoltz immediately picked up their luggage and transferred to my room. We didn't know each other at the time.

A book called *The Colonel's Lady* written by a lieutenant's wife tells about her voyage overseas aboard the US Grant. She stayed in the same stateroom Ruth, Minnie and I shared. Because of her poor rank, the woman said, she slept on the small bunk under the window. But we left our luggage on that bunk. Since the room could hold five or six people, the three of us had room to spread out. All our lives we've remained close friends. None of the six nurses ever exchanged a discordant word on the trip.

That first night on board the US Grant, I took all the corsages upstairs and asked the ship's staff to store them in the refrigerator. So then each night, the six nurses would wear a gardenia corsage to dinner. Only the nurses wore gardenia corsages. We had our flowers all the way to Hawaii.

One of the nurses, Rosemary Hogan, forewarned us about something she'd heard from other nurses. She said the ship's officers tended to enlist nurses sailing as passengers to watch the children so that parents could have freedom to enjoy the trip.

Sure enough, the ship's doctor, a captain, called the nurses to his quarters the first night for a little social hour and began to describe his plans. But he never reckoned on Rosemary Hogan, who had looked into traveling and came prepared. She informed him that we are not on duty status and would not do duty unless someone became ill and needed nursing. The rest of us sat open-mouthed as she spoke, and so did the captain.

Rosemary then pointed to a woman who was extremely

Above, on the deck of the US Grant, First Lieutenant Stephen Farris, right, chats with First Lieutenant Donald R. Snoke, who died during World War II. At right nurse Minnie Breese poses with Captain Cotter on the US Grant.

pregnant and asked why she was traveling on the ship, when the rules say women may not sail if they are within three months' of delivery. Rosemary Hogan had done her homework.

"Well, that's at the discretion of the surgeon," he answered.

So the woman sailed with us. However, she went into labor just before the US Grant pulled into Manila. She had to be taken off by a launch so she wouldn't deliver the baby on board the ship.

We did take care of female patients and soldiers who were ill, but we refused to take duty for the children as baby sitters. We only performed short stints of duty.

I always have been grateful to Rosemary Hogan because we had a wonderful time on board. We played deck games and danced, watched a movie and soaked in the sunshine on the deck. We walked around the deck during the day or relaxed in a deck chair. We made friends with many people.

We enjoyed the trip, despite a little storm here and there when the seas grew a little rough. None of the nurses became seasick, as I recall. We seemed to have simply enjoyed a very good time.

We stopped in Hawaii for two days. When we left the ship, we wore leis and I enjoyed a delightful visit with the nurses who had been at Fort Warren: Helen Locke, Martha Smith, Helene Sorenson and Marguerite Hansen. That was a very pleasant two days.

However, I was disappointed when we couldn't disembark at Guam. The night before we arrived, first one man and then another came down with a communicable disease—I can't remember if it was measles, mumps or chickenpox. So we had to stay on the ship. But soldiers from Guam visited the ship in little motorboats and passengers dropped money down to them, so they could purchase whatever for them. They returned with the items, which were hauled onto the ship.

*I enjoyed seeing my friends from Fort
Warren when the US Grant stopped
briefly in Hawaii. Pictured from left
are Marguerite Hansen, me, Helen
Locke, Martha Smith and Helene
Sorenson. Below, I am relaxing on the
deck en route to Manila.*

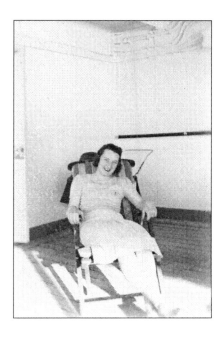

Arriving in Manila

WE ARRIVED IN MANILA BAY at night on May 18, 1940. When the ship anchored in the bay, the breezes that comforted us through the last days of tropical sailing ended. We found the sultry air stifling and the staterooms without any breathable air.

All of those able to do so drew their mattresses onto the deck so they could try to sleep. Everyone slept on the deck, attired in his or her pajamas, walking along the deck, talking and eating.

I stood at the railing, unable to sleep as I prepared for my great life adventure, and watched all the bright lights from the cars going frontward and backward on Dewey Boulevard in Manila. There came the voice of my sister Therese, who taught me to appreciate all the important events in my life. I looked at the lights and the tropical scene and recall saying: "This is it!"

A boarding party came aboard early the next morning. Friends, family and servicemen lined the dock to welcome the newcomers. I didn't expect to see anyone I knew, but then I heard: "Good God, Goldie, here I go!"

There stood Captain Goldtrap, whom I had known at Fort Warren, with his family. His shout brought to mind my first adventure on a horse called High Hat. The captain allowed me to ride his horse on a morning group ride. The horse took off at a gallop toward railroad tracks with a gravel pit on either side. As a novice, I had just learned beginning jumping. I stood and leaned forward on the horse's neck, while Captain Goldtrap forced his horse next to me. High Hat didn't stumble on the tracks but simply jumped over the ditch, at which time I yelled: "Good God, Goldie, here I go!"

The horse landed on four legs without stumbling and I couldn't believe it but I still sat on top of her. Captain Goldtrap then exchanged horses with me.

Leaving the ship, on May 19, 1940, I reported to the Philippine Department. It just happened that Minnie, Ruth and I went together to the table where officials gave

A hut made of bamboo on the island of Corregidor served as clubhouse for the Army Club.

people their new assignments. "Have you nurses been assigned?"

We hadn't. They said they had three vacancies at Fort Mills Station Hospital on Corregidor. We said, "We'll take them."

The other nurses—Rosemary Hogan and Willa Hook—went north to Stotsenberg General Hospital.

In addition to Captain Goldtrap, I also saw a dentist I knew from Fort Warren at the Army-Navy Officers' Club for the Bienvenida—welcoming party. When people left the islands, the club usually hosted a Despidada, or going-away party.

I joined the people I knew from Cheyenne and they introduced me to rum and Coca-Cola. We spent the night at the nurses' quarters at Sternberg General Hospital.

I awakened to tremendous heat and humidity—and the results of overindulging the night before.

That morning, May 20, we sailed on an inter-island boat for Corregidor—a tadpole-shaped island thirty miles from Manila that partially blocks the entrance to Manila Bay. The boat ride took two-and-a-half hours.

I felt happy with my new assignment and the fact that Minnie, Ruth and I would be together. I didn't have a clear idea of the position of Corregidor in the bay. It helped that we had each received aboard ship a 1939 pam-

I delighted in the scent of gardenia blooming from a large bush outside my bedroom at Fort Mills.

phlet on *The Harbor Defenses of Manila and Subic Bay*. It explained that Corregidor lies between "rocks" known as Fraile (friar), Monja (sleeping nun) and Mariveles, now part of the province of Bataan.

The island had about forty miles of roads and trails that a motor vehicle could travel, as well as an electric trolley car service maintained between Bottomside (the dock area) and Topside (the harbor defenses area). Six hundred feet of elevation and 3.69 miles separated the two terminals, which were divided by the Malinta Tunnel.

An ambulance and driver met us when we docked at Corregidor. Then he took us to the nurses' quarters on Middleside. The officers' club was on Topside. Later someone drove us to where we could watch the sun set. Within minutes the sun dropped from the sky.

Captain Maude Davidson, the chief nurse, welcomed us to Fort Mills. She proved to be a soft-spoken woman who had served during World War I. It didn't take any of us long to realize she meant what she said.

The nursing staff at Fort Mills totaled eight, including the chief nurse. Assigned to my own room, I discovered I would share a bathroom with Miss Josie Nesbit.

I also received a delightful surprise at my new quarters— the largest gardenia bush imaginable grew directly under my second-story room. When it bloomed, I could hardly breathe, but I found the scent heavenly.

Chapter Four

Fort Mills on Corregidor

Nursing, Acting and Socializing

Ruth Stoltz relaxes with Lieutenant Don Snoke at the Corregidor Club in April 1941, a year after arriving in the Philippines.

Life at Fort Mills on Corregidor

AS NEW NURSES, we had to follow an unwritten rule instituted in World War I that required newcomers arriving from another station to spend the first thirty days on night duty working twelve-hour shifts, with no time off. (I took note of all the orders not in writing, and that rule was the first one I changed when I became a chief nurse, so nurses received a month to know the patients and the routine before going on night duty.)

To reach the hospital, we walked straight up hundreds of stairs from the nurses' quarters, or we could follow a road that wound around the hill and up to the hospital. On nice days we walked along the road, but if it rained, we'd carry an umbrella and climb the stairs.

After completing my time on night duty, from 7 P.M. to 7 A.M., I replaced the surgery nurse on the ward. Working during the day often included working split shifts. At the time, nurses earned $90 a month.

The surgical floor was mine. Surgery duty covered a number of assignments—the operating room, surgery ward, a small officers' ward and a ward for Filipino soldiers' wives,

OFFICIAL BULLETIN

| Phones 761, 762, 763 | FRIDAY, MAY 31, 1940 | No. 128 |

1. HARBOR BOATS:

		LV CORREGIDOR		LV MANILA
TODAY -----------------	HARRISON ----	7:00 AM ------------		3:30 PM
	MILEY -------	3:30 PM ------------		10:00 AM
SATURDAY, June 1 ---	HARRISON ----	7:30 AM ------------		11:00 PM
	MILEY -------	2:00 PM ------------		9:00 AM
SUNDAY, June 2 -----	HARRISON ----	4:00 PM ------------		7:30 PM
MONDAY, June 3 -----	MILEY -------	3:30 PM ------------		10:00 AM

2. INTERIOR GUARD:

May 31:

		:DUTIES::	PHONES:	DAY	NIGHT
Capt. W. A. TODD, Jr., MC		:Med. OD:		423	428
1st Lt. J.B.F. DICE, 91st CA		:Post OD:		111	1
2nd Lt. J. H. DAVIS, 91st CA		:Post OG:		77	132
1st Lt. M.M. IRVINE, 92nd CA		:92nd OD:		296	392

June 1:

1st Lt. R. F. MOORE, CAC, Post OD.
2nd Lt. D.F. HAYNES, 60th CA, Post OG.

Reception for Incoming Officers, Cont'd.

Persons to be in the receiving line are requested to be at the Corregidor Club not later than 9:00 PM sharp, in order that they may greet General and Mrs. Wilson and take their places by 9:15 PM. Regimental Adjutants are requested to assist in the formation of the receiving line. The Secretary, Corregidor Club will arrange for music, transportation, and refreshments. The receiving line, arranged in the order in which the line will be formed, consists of:

Brig. Gen. & Mrs. Walter K. Wilson
Lt. Col. and Mrs. R.B. Murrell
Miss Eleanor F. Murrell
Mrs. William C. Doyle
Maj. and Mrs. Napoleon Boudreau
Maj. and Mrs. Edwin F. Harry
Capt. & Mrs. H Townsend Artman
Lt. Burton R. Brown
Lt. and Mrs. Phillip E. Lehr
Lt. Samuel A. Madison
Lt. Donald R. Snoke
Lt. Stephen C. Ferris
Lt. F. A. Fallmeth
Lt. Minnie L. Breese
Lt. Ruth M. Stoltz

An Officers' Reception greeted the new arrivals at Fort Mills on Corregidor May 31, less than two weeks after we arrived at Corregidor.

At left, Maude Davidson, Josie Nesbit, Ruth Stoltz and Captain Weaver are pictured at the entrance to Bilibid Prison Stockade Hospital December 29, 1940, the only visiting day each year. In the photo below, seen on a visit to Cabcabos are Captain R. Townsend Artman of the Medical Corps, Padre Coholan (Chaplain Philip F. Coholan, a lieutenant colonel) and Josie Nesbit.

which included obstetrics and gynecology.

When a Filipino woman went into labor, it was custom for family members to sleep under the bed at night to help with the language barrier. Most of the women delivered quickly and transferred right away to the delivery room. We phoned the doctor on duty. The nurse on duty scrubbed quickly and donned gloves and gown. Usually, the nurse was delivering the baby by the time the doctor arrived, gloved and gowned, in time to tie the umbilical cord. Practice made perfect, and we were fortunate that all were successful deliveries during my fourteen months on Corregidor.

I oversaw a ward of thirty patients. I would give the patients their medication, and then I'd go to surgery and scrub. When I finished in surgery, I'd return to the ward and resume my duties there.

I continued to work rotating duty on the night shift. Nurses could walk outside on the hospital's balcony while making rounds. Many a night I looked up and saw the stars of the Southern Cross, watching it change position in the sky as the hours passed.

I didn't sleep very well in the daytime. It wasn't so much temperature as humidity. We learned to cover a rubber sheet with a moist bath towel and place another moist towel on top of us.

Catholics and meatless Fridays

WHEN THE CHIEF NURSE first interviewed me, she said, "I see you give Catholic as your religion."

"Yes," I acknowledged.

"Are you a practicing one?" Captain Davidson continued. "Do you eat meat on Fridays?"

"I knowingly have not," I responded.

The first Friday on Corregidor, when dinner arrived, the seven other nurses received a plate with a meat dish while before me sat a beautifully prepared crab.

Major Weaver, seen in the photo at left, swore me into the counterespionage intelligence service while I served as a nurse at Fort Mills on Corregidor. He left the Philippines before war broke out, which ended my unsolicited life as a spy.

Minnie Breese looked at my dinner and asked: "Ma'am, why has she got that for dinner?"

Captain Davidson responded: "Because she is a practicing Catholic."

Minnie quickly stated: "Ma'am, as of now I am a practicing Catholic."

And Ruth said, "Yes, ma'am, as of now I'm a practicing Catholic too."

So, until I transferred from Corregidor, Friday dinners prepared by our Chinese cook proved to be a culinary meatless delight and a highlight of the week.

Sworn to secrecy

ONE DAY WHILE ON DUTY, after I'd been at Fort Mills for several months, a sergeant came to me and said: "Ma'am, Major Weaver asked that you come to his office."

I turned over the ward to an orderly and quickly followed the sergeant downstairs. Again, as I walked down the wide-open stairs almost floating, I knew that something out of the ordinary was in the offing.

The office door was open. When I arrived, the major—a doctor—rose.

"Please, Miss Fellmeth," Major Weaver said. "Close the door and take a seat."

He told me what he had to say must remain a secret. I must not mention it outside his office. I couldn't help but smile. I put my hands to my face. He questioned my reaction, asking, "What's wrong?"

I said: "Nothing. Only I expected you to ask me to do something unusual."

He then informed me he worked for the intelligence headquarters staff in counterespionage. He said the intelligence office singled me out to join the security team. I didn't have to accept the assignment, but I couldn't reveal this conversation to anyone.

I never considered refusing. I agreed to take the oath.

He gave me a phone number and a contact name— Shoemaker—and asked if I'd have trouble remembering it. "No," I said, "that's easy. I have a cousin by that name."

He told me the intelligence service had a number of the staff under surveillance. He then gave me names and details.

At the time, it sounded like something I could do. Later I realized that it was a terrible assignment, analyzing casual conversations for any nuances—although it seemed simple enough when explained to me in that office. But I did realize that spying isn't my forte. I didn't enjoy having to keep track of conversations or search for underlying meaning in everyday conversations.

To this day, I don't think any of the nurses knew I had agreed to serve in counterespionage. I was never permitted to tell.

A fun time for the leading lady

WE ENJOYED SWIMMING, bowling, golfing or playing badminton at the Corregidor Club. We also attended evening dances on Saturdays.

We'd have receptions at the homes of people to celebrate birthdays or other important dates.

Every year, the women's club—made up of officers' wives and families—sponsored a stage production.

One evening, the nurses—including Captain Davidson—and I planned to go Topside to see a movie on "Wally's date money," which he sent to me every month.

I had read a bulletin about the dates and times for tryouts for the upcoming play, so at the dinner table I suggested: "Let's go to the play tryouts and see if we can participate in the play."

The other nurses greeted my suggestion at first with surprise, then dismay.

But I persuaded them it would be something different to do. We might be able to help with props, costumes or wardrobes. "Why not? We could help and have fun," I said.

So a group of us attended the tryouts and, while there, we had been given copies of the play. The director— the warrant officer's wife who had studied drama in Boston or at Julliard—looked over at the nurses and asked, "Wouldn't one of you like to try out?"

The others quickly responded: "No." Before I realized what I was doing, I raised my hand and said, "I'd like to try out for a part."

My father—a very dignified man who looked like Louis Stone—had started a little theatre group in Chicago at our parish and for more than thirty years he directed four performances a year. I remember rummaging through trunks of costumes stored in our attic. Once or twice I performed a small part, but I found acting very natural.

After a brief interview, the director said, "Try the lead."

I played the leading female role in "Personal Appearance," a play performed by the Corregidor Players. I am seen in the top photo with the leading man, Lieutenant Spengler, and at left during the performance. In the play, the main character is an actress with a beautiful coiffure that is referred to only as "that color hair." So I used a henna rinse to change my brown locks to red.

News from the "Rock"

At the second try-out for the Corregidor Player's coming Production, "Personal Appearance", the cast was selected. The leading lady, Carole Arden, is to be played by Miss Floramund Fellmeth—this part was taken by Gladys George in the original stage production. The other female parts are to be played by Mrs. Harry Julian as Joyce Struthers—the young fiancee, Mrs. L. A. Bosworth as Gladys Kelcey—the movie struck ingenue. Mrs. Lloyd E. Mielenz will take the part of Mrs. Struthers who has delusions of grandeur. Ralph E. Murrell as Aunt Kate Barnahy—a comical old maid. Mrs. George Crawford as Jessie—Carole Arden's French maid. In the male parts we have Lieutenant Burton R. Brown as Bud Norton—leading juvenile character a rather home chap who can't be led by the movie people. Lieutenant Henry M. Spengle will take the part of Gilbert Gordon—who appears in the movie which is the beginning of the play. Mr. William H. Hankin as Clyde Pelton the mechanic assistant, Lieutenant Harry Julian will play Gene Tuttle—Miss Arden's press agent, and Lieutenant James R. Holmes as Johnson, the chauffeur. Directing the play will be Mrs. M. F. Schmidt assisted by Mrs. Clair McK. Congelman, stage manager will be Lieutenant H. M. Splengler, Mrs. Robert P. Glassburn in charge of properties, Costumes—Mrs. Betty M. Doyle, Make-up—Miss Penelope Mielenz and Mr. William H. Hankin. For the movie which opens the play the advisors will be Mrs. Willis Shippam and Major William B. Short.

Major Napoleon Boudreau has been promoted to Lieutenant Colonel effective July 13, 1940.

I received notoriety in the Corregidor newspaper for being selected to play the leading role in the Corregidor Players' performance of "Personal Appearance." Years later at a reunion of the Defenders of Bataan and Corregidor, one of the soldiers asked whatever happened to that red-headed nurse—me after my henna rinse!

```
                                        October 6, 1940.


  Miss Floramund A. Fellmeth,
       Fort Mills, P. I.

  My dear Miss Fellmeth:

            On Friday evening, October 4, 1940, at the
  Topside Cine, it was my great pleasure to witness your
  excellent characterization of Carole Arden in the Riley
  Comedy "Personal Appearance."

            The manner in which you captivated and held
  the unusually large audience indicates the splendid
  histrionic abilities which you displayed. The garrison
  is unanimous in its praise of your work and joins me in
  thanking you for the time and talent you contributed.

            Very sincerely,


                              WALTER K. WILSON,
                           Brigadier General, U.S.A.,
                                 Commanding.
```

*I received a letter of congratulations after my performance in the play
from Walter K. Wilson, Brigadier General.*

The play was called "Personal Appearance." I read the
part and did what they told me to do.

After my audition, we thanked the director and left. We
went to watch a movie and, after the film, as we left the
stone entrance to the theater, I heard someone say:
"Leading lady—oh, leading lady. Congratulations leading
lady."

I turned and looked in surprise at the general's aide,
Captain Brown. "You haven't heard?" he asked, embarrassed. "Didn't you know you have the part? Miss
Fellmeth is the leading lady." Well, I didn't know, but I
enjoyed it.

Practicing for the play changed daily life at the nurses'
quarters. One of the older nurses, who left before the war
began, insisted: "Well, you're going to have to recite for
me every day and, unless I know that you do it well, I'm

not going to go to watch the show."

In the play, characters refer to the leading lady's locks as "that color hair." I went to Manila seeking a blond wig to cover my brown hair, but the wigs proved inadequate.

So, I told the chief nurse, "In the summer, if I'm in the sun, my hair becomes auburn. Why don't I go each week and have them give me a henna rinse?"

In three weeks my hair slowly changed to a nice shade of auburn. (In fact, years later at a reunion of the Defenders of Bataan and Corregidor, an ex-POW asked one of the nurses: "Whatever happened to that redheaded nurse from Corregidor?" She pointed to me and said, "She's right over there but she's not a redhead.")

We performed the play at the Topsice Cine before packed audiences. Instead of one show, we performed the play three times so everyone who wanted to attend could do so. I have a beautiful personal congratulatory note that the base commander, Brigadier General Walter K. Wilson, sent to me after seeing the play.

The general wrote:

"My dear Miss Fellmeth:

"On Friday evening, October 4, 1940, at the Topside Cine, it was my great pleasure to witness your excellent characterization of Carole Arden in the Riley Comedy "Personal Appearance."

"The manner in which you captivated and held the unusually large audience indicates the splendid histrionic abilities which you displayed. The garrison is unanimous in its praise of your work and joins me in thanking you for the time and talent you contributed."

A treasure hunt

WHILE WE ENJOYED THE SOCIAL LIFE, we also heard constant rumors of war coming to the Islands—espe-

Some of the nurses are dressed for the evening at Corregidor in 1940.
I am seen at left, next to V. Ferguson, Minnie Breese and Ruth Stoltz.
Below, I climbed to the end of one of these big guns, reached inside the
barrel and discovered the treasure—a bag of pennies!
> —Photo below courtesy of Corregidor Historic Society.

*Searching for treasure in the dark
of night, I remember seeing car
headlights flash against tree trunks
as we drove along the roads, such as
Middleside Road, pictured above. Wally
and I returned to the Philippine Islands
in the mid-1980s and saw again the
guns at Battery Way where
I found the treasure.*

—The photo below is courtesy of
the Corregidor Historic Society.

cially after the Army ordered the wives and families of military officers to return to the United States in May 1941. Some chose to stay in Manila. Since they weren't military per se, nobody could make them leave. They later became prisoners of war.

After the wives had left, the officers often devised recreational activities. One time they planned a progressive treasure hunt.

First we enjoyed a buffet supper. Then each of the nurses rode with a group of the men. Inside each car, passengers received a slip of paper with cryptic instructions that led them from one to ten different places on the island.

In preparation for a coming war, everything remained in darkness on Corregidor, and you could see only by the headlights of the cars. Everyone followed one another, driving up and down the small island, searching for clues and the treasure!

By flashlight we read and deciphered the four cleverly written lines that led us to the next clue. Each car raced from one clue to the next, trying to reach the site before the others.

The last sheet directed us to a big gun battery.

Although I wore a blouse and a long black skirt with high heels, when we arrived at the gun battery we climbed down inside the dark belowground gun placement. Looking around, it dawned on me that the trophy might be in the barrel of the gun. I directed an officer to "Boost me. Lift me up on the gun." He didn't want to, but I persuaded him.

I never could have done such a thing in daylight because I dislike heights, but as it was dark, I straddled the huge, elevated gun and worked my way to the muzzle. I pulled back a section of canvas covering the opening, then stuck my hand inside, feeling around until I found it—the very heavy prize—a bag of copper pennies! In fact, it proved to be a very large bag of copper pennies—a treasure!

"I've got it," I cried, as I scooted back down the gun barrel. "Get me off this!"

While on Corregidor, I helped stock medicine and food in the Malinta Tunnel as part of an emergency drill. Above is the Malinta Tunnel as seen in the 1980s. In the photo at left, I can be seen at the far left in my white uniform, helping to move equipment in June 1941, with First Lieutenant John Haines and Captain R. Townsend Artman in the foreground. Below, other workers load supplies into an ambulance for transport to the tunnel.

The other groups began arriving at this point so we rushed to the starting point. The other contestants saw us leave, realizing we had the trophy and following in hopes of cutting us off and capturing the prize for themselves. I remember seeing headlights flash on trees as cars drove through the dark of night.

By the time the others arrived, I sat on the living room floor dividing a mountain of copper pennies. Our trophy!

The serious side

L IFE ON CORREGIDOR had its serious side as well. Although the wives and families had been ordered home, I do not believe anyone in the Philippine Islands doubted that reinforcements would arrive to bring a quick and victorious end to the Japanese threat.

In preparation, we held maneuvers and field operations. We moved litters, crates and boxes of supplies from the hospital down to Malinta Tunnel.

After the war, when I mentioned helping to stock the Malinta Tunnel with supplies, Hattie "HR" Brantley said: "Well, you didn't put enough in there." But how could we know how long American and Filipino forces would seek shelter inside the tunnel from Japanese invaders?

It took ten years for the Americans to build the 835-foot-long tunnel, which stretched twenty-four feet wide and eighteen feet high. They finished the concrete-reinforced tunnel in 1932, anticipating stocking it with ammunition, food and supplies. The medical staff at Fort Mills started stocking it for use as a 1,000-bed hospital in case of war.

We also suffered through earthquakes. We had been taught to stand in doorways during earthquakes. One time, Ruth Stoltz and I had been on night duty so we were sleeping when the earth started rumbling. Our buildings stood next to each other and we kept the large windows open.

I called to Ruth, "Are you OK?"

"Yes," she responded. When the shaking stopped, I heard Ruth laughing.

Dear Nurse,
I am afraid
    and lone
        I cry,
until
    your wisp
    of white
        floats by.

For as you go
you take
    my fear,
    since now
    I know
        your care
        is near...

A poem by
Wynona
Bice-
Stephens
from her
book, *The Art
of Nursing*

"What's wrong?" I asked.

"My two (small) cloisonné vases were shaking, standing on my chest of drawers. Instead of removing them, I stood next to the chest and held them on their stands—instead of just removing them!"

After the war, I reminded her of the incident. "I still have them," she told me. I presume like many of us, she sent the vases home with many of her other possessions before the war began.

Preparing to return home

AS NURSES NEARED THE END of their two years in the Philippines, most transferred to Manila so they could explore more of the islands, such as the bat caves, festivals and other items of interest. After fourteen months on Corregidor, I transferred to Fort McKinley, which sat eight kilometers outside of Manila.

I left Corregidor July 1, 1941. Both Josie Nesbit and Maude Davison had already transferred to the mainland.

When the families left, the Army allowed us to send items home. I wasn't due to go home until May 1942, but I had bought items at Corregidor and Manila that I hoped to save. I had purchased tablecloths, a Chinese chest, a beautiful Indian teak screen and many other items.

From what I've learned later, it's amazing my possessions arrived in Chicago. The ship had a near-miss in Hawaii and, although it didn't sink, it had been debilitated. Everything aboard the ship wound up spread throughout the United States.

My sister Colette told me about when my trunks arrived on New Year's Eve, just before the advent of 1942. As everyone gathered at home, preparing to celebrate the New Year, a harried truck driver working overtime in the cold and snow pulled up to the house and just dumped my boxes outside. The family brought the boxes inside—a teak chest and a box containing china, linens and papers. Everything smelled of mothballs! They described it as

Captain William Stryker is seen going down the steps outside the Fort Mills hospital heading toward Malinta Tunnel, where medical workers stocked supplies for use in emergencies. Below is a view of a balcony that surrounded the wards of Station Hospital on Corregidor in January 1941. I used to see the Southern Cross while making my rounds at night.

perfect timing. My sister-in-law's brother was serving in Europe, I was overseas at Manila and all the families at the house had someone they knew serving abroad.

In April 1941, I visited
Mariveles on Bataan, above,
where I saw huts and boats
along the beach. At left, I
pause on a dock during the
trip. Below, Below, Ruth
Stoltz is seen on Bottomside
after we received a ride in a
banca boat in January 1941.

Chapter Five

War Descends on Paradise

Dodging Bombs and Treating Wounded

At Fort McKinley, I shared a bungalow with Hattie "H.R." Brantley (top right), Earleen Allen, (bottom left) and Mary Jo Oberst (bottom right).

Life at Fort McKinley

ON JULY 1, 1941, I arrived at Fort William McKinley seven miles southeast of Manila. I had requested transfer to the mainland and the Army assigned me to Fort McKinley.

I shared a nice little four-bedroom cottage with Hattie "H.R." Brantley, Earleen Allen and Mary Jo Oberst. We had separate bedrooms but a common living room and kitchenette. Fortunately, we all lived together pleasantly.

The chief nurse, First Lieutenant Eleanor E. O'Neill, had come down from Stotsenburg to set up the clinic as a hospital. She already had a surgical nurse when I arrived, so I went out on the floor.

Josie had been transferred to Sternberg Hospital, along with Maude Davison, who was my chief nurse on Corregidor.

While on duty, I fell extremely ill for eleven days with dengue fever, also called break-bone fever, which is transmitted by mosquitoes. Tiny veins in your calves below the knees just rupture.

Symptoms include a fever, painful headaches, a rash and pain in the eyes, joints and muscles. I ran a high temperature for days and spent time as a patient in the hospital.

I was transported August 28 to Sternberg General Hospital in Manila, where I stayed in the hospital until September 8. I returned to duty on September 9.

I felt well for a week and then fell ill again September 20 for another fifteen days, till the fever ran its course. Then I received a sixteen-day leave from Sternberg General Hospital, when I traveled with Ruth Stoltz to Baguio, a cooler, hilly region of the tropical islands with brooks, forests and the Baguio Country Club, which sported a golf course and offered rest and relaxation to Americans in the Philippines.

Dinners, parties and games

WHEN I TRANSFERRED TO FORT MCKINLEY, my counterespionage assignment followed me.

A date took me to a German restaurant, where only a few other people were dining. He ordered steak and I ordered roasted veal knuckle and red kraut for dinner.

When the meal arrived, I could eat only perhaps a quarter of the huge portion so, although it embarrassed my escort, I asked the German woman if she had a container I could use to take the remainder back to my quarters. She came out with a big brown bag, having added dumplings and

In October 1941, I dressed as the Queen of the May to attend a Thwarted Ambitions party with Navy officers and nurses from the Cavite Naval Base. Pictured above (with last names only) are Vivanku, Richardson, Fellmeth (standing third from the right), Fabian and Lietwiller standing, and seated are McCellan, Army nurse Earlyn Black and Taylor.

red cabbage to the roast inside the bag.

The following day, someone called me on the phone and asked: "Did you enjoy your veal knuckle?"

I brought the leftovers home and tucked the bag into the refrigerator. I worked the next day and when I came off duty at three o'clock, I looked forward to eating the rest of my veal and dumplings! I walked into the house only to find our small living room crowded with my three house-mates and my date from the night before, as well as other officers. They had eaten all of my leftovers!

Noting my disappointment, and feeling I deserved recompense, a few went off to the commissary to buy snacks. They returned with rye bread, cold cuts, sausage, cheese and beer. As we ate, the evening finished with a discussion of gun mounts. The officers worked out ideas using upside down chairs. I later recalled that evening when our first flyers on fighter planes developed methods of mounting guns onto their planes.

Another time, in October 1941, five Navy officers and one Navy nurse from the Cavite Naval Base came to a Thwarted Ambitions Party, where everyone dressed as someone they'd like to have been. I went as the Queen of the May. At another party I met Edwina Todd, a Navy nurse I kept in touch with throughout the years.

In November 1941, we enjoyed the Army-Navy game. Later I saw the movie, *The Winds of War*, and a Navy cadet rode the mule, but in Manila Floramund Anna Fellmeth rode the mule. I had charged the dress I wore that night. After the war, I received the bill and paid for it.

Preparing for war

EVERYONE FELT A BIT ON EDGE as the Philippine Islands prepared for a war that seemed inevitable. During the late fall of 1941, no one was permitted off the base for more than thirty minutes without signing out and everyone had to give a destination.

Each nurse was issued a World War I gas mask and a helmet. We tested our masks inside a big tent outside the hospital. Periodically, we removed the masks, and when our arms started stinging and we couldn't breathe because of the gas, we were told to leave the tents. I have a receipt showing I received a gas mask in May 1941, six months before the bombing of Pearl Harbor.

We each received metal discs with a hole in the end and molds of letters. Using a hammer, each nurse pounded the letters of her name into the metal, creating nametags or "dog" tags. We wore them all the time and never did replace them. I still have my dog tags, held together with an old yellowed string.

Anticipating the Japanese might attack, the military issued World War I gas masks to the nurses in May 1941, as indicated by the date on the issue slip below. Two weeks before the first bombing raid, the nurses tested their masks in a tent, as seen above. At left, I am seen wearing my WWI gas mask.

The first night raid

IBELIEVE I WAS ON DUTY when I heard about the bombing of our ships at Pearl Harbor, which occurred December 7 in the States and December 8 in the Philippines. Of course, at that time we didn't know it as Pearl Harbor—just our base in Hawaii. Even my mother in Chicago had to ask: "Where's Pearl Harbor?"

We heard the news about 6:30 the morning of December 8. At first, we all thought it must be yet another rumor. We had known about the war in Europe and Tokyo Rose broadcast strange stories so we sometimes had trouble separating fact from fiction, rumors from truth. Rumors had been rampant since the families had been sent home more than six months earlier. And we always figured we'd receive help. It never occurred to anyone that we'd stay in the Philippines and lose!

We went about our duties as usual, but from that moment on, we wondered when the Japanese would attack the islands.

We didn't have long to wait.

The first bombing occurred up north that afternoon, December 8, when fifty-four twin-motored Mitsubishi bombers attacked Clark Field, followed by dozens of Zero fighters who shot .50-caliber bullets that destroyed planes and killed people on the ground during strafing attacks.

The following night—shortly after 3 A.M. December 9— Japanese bombers attacked Nichols Air Field near Fort McKinley.

In the middle of that bright moonlit night, the heavens opened and the earth rumbled as Japanese bombs hit the ground and exploded.

I awakened to the sound of a blast on the road in front of our bungalow. The tracer bullets made us—H.R. Brantley, Earleen Allen, Mary Jo Oberst and me—feel as if we sat in the center of a massive fireworks display, with bright flashes shooting from the heavens and earth. We heard a constant "ack—ack" resounding from guns fired at the invading planes. The earth vibrated.

No one had told us what to do in the event of an attack. Without any discussion, the four of us left our rooms and rushed down the six steps of the porch and headed for the filthy dirt floor underneath.

I found myself in my special rayon nightgown under the porch—I do not recall now if it was pink or blue—with one white stocking on and the other in my hand. Wooden lattice enclosed the side of the porch.

A few minutes later a group of Filipino soldiers joined us. They were very excited and kept repeating: "A bomb, Mum (ma'am)!" They'd seen it drop from a Japanese plane, but in the daylight it proved to be an empty fuel tank.

I reacted by asking: "Do you want me to pray?" I do not remember whether I waited for an answer before I started to pray the *Our Father* (also known as *The Lord's Prayer*). When all was quiet, we climbed out from beneath the porch and went inside.

Back in our house, one of the nurses asked whether we should go to the hospital. Without giving it a second thought, I responded: "No. I think they will call us if we are needed."

So we went back to bed and, believe it or not, we slept.

We awakened at our normal time the next morning, dressed and walked to the hospital mess hall, only to find chaos and wounded everywhere. We were instructed to eat breakfast and report to our wards. I went to surgery. We were the relief everyone needed. My decision of the night proved correct.

When I reported to the operating room, I beheld a horrible sight. I recognized the first patient I saw on the surgical table—a soldier with a large cast whom we had discharged a few days earlier after a minor surgery. I had just treated him! I looked at him and said: "What are you doing here? I just released you to duty." He said, "Hello, ma'am." I saw him again when we both sailed aboard the Mactan.

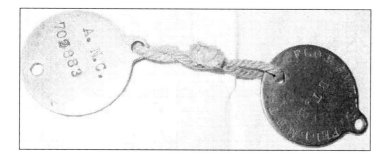

I used a hammer to pound my name onto metal discs with a hole on the end, which served as my "dog" tags throughout the war. The nurses wore the tags all the time.

Life in a war zone

THE JAPANESE RAIDS CONTINUED day and night. The very next night another raid awakened us. Fifteen minutes after a bombing, patients arrived en masse at the hospital. The nurses kept working as usual, other than swapping our white uniforms for men's khaki slacks and shirts.

Officials at the two-story wooden hospital instructed the staff during air raids to evacuate all ambulatory patients to the basement. While the basement helped during the strafing, it would have offered little protection if a bomb had directly hit the hospital. The staff also released all patients from traction and placed them under their beds.

Only the U.S. military sense of humor alleviated the tension.

During one raid, as I walked down the stairs to the basement, I mentioned, "Oh, I could do with a glass of water." Not long afterward, an orderly arrived with a pitcher of water and one glass.

"One glass?" I commented.

He answered: "From now on, ma'am, we don't have to worry about germs."

We all drank from one glass.

During another air raid, when I was the only nurse left on the ward with the patients in traction, one of the men refused to be released from traction and placed under his bed.

As explosions sounded outside, I heard the patient next to him ask: "Why don't you want to be moved under your bed?"

The man lying on his bed answered: "I am not worried because if the bomb doesn't have your name on it, you won't get hit."

The man on the floor responded: "That's not the one worrying me. It's the one that says—'To Whom It May Concern.'"

A good laugh prompted by clean, spontaneous humor made trying moments tolerable. On the whole, our great American sense of humor carried us through many, many tight spots.

Bombs never struck the hospital.

When it looked like reinforcements wouldn't arrive, the U.S. troops started destroying supplies to keep them from falling into enemy hands. So we'd hear heavy explosions and see fires everywhere. We'd glimpse the fires, but we were always too busy to stand and watch. Fifteen minutes after a raid, patients poured into the hospital.

Dancing with officers

ONE DAY I REMEMBER three officer friends of mine asked me to accompany them to the Manila Hotel to hear a band play. I wasn't dating them; we were just friends. The hotel had a pool and dance floor. We took turns dancing.

I finally had to slip my shoes off. We danced till two or three in the morning. Then they took me back to Fort McKinley because I had to work in surgery in the morning.

The next day, I came off duty to find them on my

The Directory of All Officers stationed within the Philippine Department, July 16, 1941 edition, *lists General Douglas MacArthur as well as Major Sam Lamb, a man I dated in the Philippines. Wally and I obtained a copy of the directory from the national archives.*

doorstep with the request: "Let's go dancing." I danced and I ate and I danced! I told them, "Oh, we can't do this anymore!" I felt so tired. I'd worked my shift at the hospital, then danced the night away with these officers. I slept only a few hours and then returned to work at the hospital.

The third day, when I came off duty, no one greeted me. I knew they were gone. That was not a nice moment.

At that time, we still all believed the United States would send us help. We were going to receive help. It proved to be a big morale booster. But there wasn't any help.

Evacuating Fort McKinley

PLANES FLEW OVER DROPPING THEIR BOMBS at all hours of the day and night. As the evacuation around Manila progressed, the number of nurses dwindled. Rumors ran rampant. Our patient load had slowed and we heard that the Japanese had landed and were headed our way.

On December 16, I was called to the office and given orders to change into slacks, carry a gas mask and fill a musette bag because I was going out with a medical team into the field. I hadn't been trained for fieldwork, but it seemed quite exciting.

I stood at the screen front door near the porch waiting and a car stopped. I recognized the officer, who came in and asked what I was doing, dressed as I was. I told him about my new assignment, and he said that if I should find myself separated from the unit, I should take refuge in an underground headquarters on the base. I didn't know till then that an underground headquarters existed at Fort McKinley.

I asked him, "Will troops be arriving from the States?" He said no.

Before I could leave for the field, the other nurses arrived at the house. We had been ordered to pack our clothes (one bag and a musette bag) and leave for Sternberg General Hospital in Manila.

The top photo shows the Carabao Gate at Fort William McKinley. The second photo shows Eagle Gate at the north end of Fort William McKinley.
—Photos courtesy of the Battling Bastards of Bataan

Earleen Allen's close friend had left his car with us so the four of us loaded it with our bags.

As the other three waited in the car, I stood on the porch and stopped.

"Come on!" Hattie called. "Hurry!"

As we drove away, Hattie asked me why I took so long.

"I was trying to decide whether or not I should lock the door," I answered. Talk about reality in the unreal—what a thought! I left the door unlocked; otherwise the Japanese would break down the door.

We drove away from Fort McKinley and checked in at Sternberg Hospital in Manila.

Willa Hook did not appreciate the levity when she saw me laughing with some military men after a Japanese bombing raid.

Dodging bullets

EVERY DAY THE BOMBING of Manila continued. As the alarms sounded, ambulatory patients hurried out to the V-slit trenches dug throughout the hospital grounds for protection during air raids. Ideally, we could watch a plane and move if necessary to the opposite side.

During one raid, I picked up a book from a table as I left the hospital. I arrived at a trench to find Willa Hook there before me. I then proceeded to read out loud: "Oh, death, thou fickle woman."

This upset Willa so I stopped reading and went back inside the hospital. I came to a lead-lined X-ray room and crawled under the table and stretched out. With my helmet halfway on my head and my gas mask next to me, believe it or not, I dozed off to sleep because we had worked through the night.

When a tremendous blast shook the building, I was hit from both sides by a captain and four corpsmen attempting to duck under the table.

I called out: "Get off of me! I can't breathe!"

When all quieted down, we walked down the corridor laughing. Coming toward us we saw Willa Hook.

"What was so funny?" she asked, angered by our laughter.

The captain answered: "Miss Fellmeth and five men attempting to get under one table!"

Philippine Women's University

My NEXT TRANSFER was to the Philippine Women's University, which had been converted to Annex D of Sternberg General Hospital. The gymnasium had been set up with ten operating tables, other tables and portable sterilizing units.

I do not know how on the spur of the moment I could have handled this but for the training I received while in the emergency room at Bellevue Hospital in New York, where ambulances arrived every five minutes and we assessed patients and then passed them on for treatment.

By the time civilian doctors and nurses arrived, our military corpsmen under my direction had lined tables straight in a row, which became our extra instrument tables. At each of the ten operating room instrument tables we placed one set of basic instruments, wastebaskets and a rinse bucket. In the adjacent room, portable sterilizers cleaned instruments and sterilized them so they could be used again.

After a devastating time, once again action slowed.

We worked for a week at the Philippine Women's University makeshift hospital. I scarcely remember sleeping or eating. I'm sure I must have eaten. I must have slept. Sleep comes naturally, so I'm very fortunate. The specifics of daily eating and sleeping just remain unclear to this day.

We heard rumors and more rumors. Bombings slowed as Japanese soldiers approached the outskirts of Manila. While we cared for the wounded, the military personnel started evacuating the city and destroying anything vital they could not take with them to Bataan or Corregidor.

Every night at midnight, ambulances rolled to the hospital doors and the staff would load the patients who, accompanied by some nurses and orderlies, left for Bataan, and from there some would travel to Corregidor. The nurses and staff set up jungle Hospital No. 1 at Limay on Bataan and Hospital No. 2 at Cabcaben south of Bataan Field.

Dear Nurse,
If clouds
    are the
        pillows
            of angels
and raindrops
    are tears
        that they
            shed,
when
    the rain
        empties all
            of the
                pillows
can
    an angel
        still rest
            her head...?

A poem by Wynona Bice-Stephens from her book, *The Art of Nursing*

A Christmas to remember

DESPITE THE CONTINUOUS BOMBING and gunfire, Christmas was approaching and my thoughts turned to a Christmas tree. Around noon on Christmas Eve, I floored the acting surgeon—a doctor with the rank of captain—by asking permission to go into the city center to buy a Christmas tree. Reluctantly, he gave permission for me to have a military car with a Filipino driver to take me into Manila.

We stopped at the city's largest department store, which is small by American standards. I entered the deserted establishment.

When a man came to wait on us, I said: "Please, we want to buy a Christmas tree."

I never will forget the look of utter disbelief on his face when he heard my request. He had weathered shelling, bombing, strafing fire … and now received a request for a Christmas tree.

After moments of astonished silence, he told me he'd look downstairs. He returned with a small, dirty artificial tree, but it would have to do. We settled on a price and I purchased it.

On our way back, we had reached a large bridge when the air raid warning siren sounded. The frightened driver pulled over in front of a small wooden store so we could take shelter inside. I suggested that we'd be better off trying to reach the college hospital, and he said: "Yes, Mum." We sped across the bridge and raced back to Annex D.

The astonished captain just stood shaking his head as I went to the operating room and confiscated a roll of cotton batting, then proceeded to set up the tree on a table in the entryway. I draped the cotton batting around the base and then arranged a set of small ceramic figurines in winter clothing, some wearing skates or riding on sleds. My family had sent me the figurines; later I regretted having to leave them behind.

After dark on Christmas Eve, a group of Jesuit students from the seminary at Santa Scholastica came to the hospi-

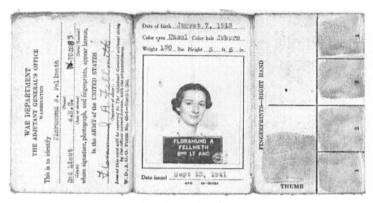

My War Department trifold identification card stated my name, rank and serial number, and included my description, photo and fingerprints.

tal and began singing Christmas carols. As the seminarians sang "Silent Night, Holy Night," the words echoed in the quiet night.

Nurses evacuated to Bataan

GRADUALLY, THE NUMBER OF PATIENTS at the university's hospital diminished. Then, on December 26—when General MacArthur withdrew his troops to Bataan—we received orders to evacuate Annex D, where we had set up only a week before, and move to Sternberg.

After loading ambulances with patients, the remaining nurses prepared to evacuate in the dark moonless night. The phone rang. A medical captain—the doctor in charge—answered the call, then returned to where the nurses stood near the ambulances.

He addressed his remarks to Lieutenant O'Neill, the chief nurse.

"Miss O'Neill," he said. "I've just had a call. One nurse has to stay behind here."

Silence greeted his remark.

"Miss O'Neill?" he repeated. "Would you please select a nurse?"

The lieutenant didn't respond. She never said a word.

Looking around in the darkness, the captain called out: "OK, Miss Fellmeth, you stay behind."

The other nurses boarded the ambulances for the trip to Bataan, while I returned to the hospital.

The captain said that, in the dark, he thought I was standing next to him. He told me he regretted having to make the decision because with the Japanese so near, he did not know if we would be able to evacuate to Manila in time.

After a restless night of sleep, I came down to the lobby in the morning for breakfast. When they saw me, one of the Filipino student nurses called out: "See, they're not all gone! They're not all gone!"

Two days after Christmas, the order came for me to transfer to Sternberg, a hospital on the banks of Manila's Pasig River. I had asked Sister Georgia, one of the Maryknoll nuns who quickly became my friend, if I could have my clothes laundered. She said she would take care of them.

The next day, I asked for transportation back to the university so I could retrieve my uniform and other clothes. I told officials I needed to return to the women's university because "I haven't any change of clothes."

When I walked in, Sister Georgia met me with outstretched hands and we exchanged news. She retrieved

Upon returning to Sternberg Hospital, I met with Colonel Percy J. Carroll, who asked if I would volunteer to sail aboard the Red Cross hospital ship, the Mactan.

my clothes, then asked where I was headed.

"I do not know where I'm going," I responded, "but I am not going with the others."

Again, somehow I knew I wouldn't be accompanying the other nurses.

When I returned to Sternberg, the main army hospital in Manila overflowing with wounded soldiers, I saw my former roommate Josie Nesbit. The first thing I said was: "Oh, Josie—we're going to go back home! We're going to Corregidor!"

Josie responded: "Well, I don't know. You're to go see Colonel Carroll."

I didn't know Colonel Percy Carroll, the senior surgeon in Manila who had served previously at the 350-bed Stotsenburg Station Hospital near Clark Field. And I had no idea then that Josie had been part of a meeting with the colonel and another senior nurse, Florence MacDonald.

I had never met Col. Percy J. Carroll when I was told to report to his office at Sternberg General Hospital. He asked me then if I would serve as the chief nurse aboard the hospital ship Mactan. I agreed. He is seen in this photo at his desk in Australia.

A chat with Colonel Carroll

I HAD SEEN COLONEL PERCY J. CARROLL (later known as General Carroll) only one time previously, but I was not acquainted with him. As I walked to his office, once again I knew something special would occur.

Although less than average in height, the colonel had an athlete's stature and a reputation for sternness. He wore a trim mustache that matched his wiry black hair, which was speckled with gray.

Colonel Carroll asked me to close the door and sit down. The commanding officer of Manila Hospital Center, a veteran of three wars, told me to raise my right hand and swear not to repeat anything I was about to hear. I did as he asked, looking into his piercing dark eyes.

He then told me that General MacArthur, working under the auspices of the Red Cross, wanted to evacuate as many patients as possible aboard an inter-island coconut husk steamer called the Mactan. He said one Army surgeon and one Army nurse would accompany the wounded soldiers and oversee ten Philippine Islands Red Cross nurses as well as a half dozen Filipino doctors. The colonel said he needed a surgical nurse who could improvise when necessary.

(I never knew how I had been selected until Florence MacDonald's evacuation to Australia, when she confided in me that she had been in the selection group. She said she prayed that I would forgive her. But the colonel had told Josie, Florence and another senior nurse he needed a trained surgical nurse for this special assignment—a competent nurse who could improvise and keep calm during emergencies. The nurse he had worked with at Stotsenberg already had been evacuated to Bataan or Corregidor. But Josie described me to him as "an outstanding surgical nurse" and MacDonald said she'd heard about me too.)

Colonel Carroll then told me the assignment was voluntary. There was no guarantee that anyone would make it to Australia.

"You don't have to take this assignment," he said. "You don't have to go."

"Are you going?" I asked him.

"Yes," the colonel answered.

I replied: "Then, sir, I will go, too." It never really entered my mind to refuse, as we were accustomed to following orders.

He told me I needed to keep silent about the plans, but my task would be to prepare a surgery on board the ship for thirty days for 300 patients. I told Colonel Carroll that I would need help from a nurse and two or three corpsman, and he agreed. He warned me again not to say anything about the plans.

I never did understand why we needed so much secrecy, unless it stemmed from the overly zealous counterespionage efforts. I know police patrolled the streets of Manila during night raids, popping off pistol shots into windows with lights illuminated or shades raised.

When I left his room, I saw a nurse I didn't know standing

outside so I asked: "How would you like to help me?" She agreed, so the two of us proceeded to select the items I would need in the surgery. Two enlisted men packed the items into boxes and sent them to the yard. We selected surgical instruments, sterile packs and other boxes of supplies, which the corpsmen carried into the yard in sealed unmarked boxes.

As we prepared the boxes, the nurse helping me (I can't recall her name) hopped onto a box, kicked her heels, hit the sides as if beating a drum—boom, boom—and chanted: "I am going wherever these boxes are going. I am going where these boxes are going."

I responded: "You want to bet?"

"Where are they going?" she asked.

"Well, I'm sorry, I can't tell you that," I responded. "But I don't think you're going with the boxes."

Between 11 A.M. and 6 P.M., the four of us put together complete surgical supplies for the trip. Other people collected beds and packed linens while a medical colonel gathered the medicines. Unfortunately, none of the boxes had been marked, so on board the Mactan we could not identify their contents without opening them.

Alone in the nurses' quarters

AT MIDNIGHT DECEMBER 28, 1941, the phone rang on the first floor of the darkened nurses' quarters. In my mosquito-netted bed, I heard Josie Nesbit answering the call. She then went to the rooms of the remaining nine nurses and awakened them for evacuation to Corregidor. She had been instructed not to disturb Miss Fellmeth.

As Josie passed my room, I called to her and she came to me. I extended my hand from under the netting and she squeezed it. We uttered not a word. Then she left.

Outside the building, through the high window in the small bedroom covered only with a net mosquito screen, I heard the nurses whispering to one another: "Why isn't she coming with us?"

For three days and nights, I remained alone in the large nurses' quarters at Sternberg General Hospital while the Mactan was converted from an inter-island steamer to a Red Cross hospital ship.
—Photo is from the Armed Forces Institute of Pathology

Josie answered: "I do not know." But she did know. She had been in on the meeting in Colonel Carroll's office when they decided which nurse to assign to the Mactan.

As the sound of traffic disappeared, I laid on my abdomen with my face in my pillow and a hand tucked under my face. I kept repeating: "I won't think. I won't think. I won't think." As our troops continued blasting supplies throughout Manila, I fell asleep.

(Josie told me later that when the nurses arrived at the Corregidor docks aboard the Don Esteban, the air raid alert sounded. Josie was carrying a large cardboard box with all the nurses' records and a colonel told her to drop the box and take cover. When she protested, he threw the precious box to the ground and hustled her into his jeep before driving to the Malinta Tunnel. When the all clear sounded, he drove her to the dock and Josie heaved a huge sigh of relief as she retrieved the box with all the nurses' important 201 records listing past assignments, serial numbers, absences and new posts. Josie then hitched a ride to the Malinta Tunnel Hospital, which she and I had helped stock during emergency drills while still living at Fort Mills.)

When the sun rose the next morning, so did I—only to realize how alone I felt as the only nurse left in the huge two-story Sternberg Hospital nurses' quarters. I went downstairs and shocked a Filipino girl working in the kitchen. Amazed at seeing me, she said she'd prepare a breakfast.

I didn't have any assigned duties. So I waited. For three days and nights I waited. While the Japanese encircled Manila—now an open city—I waited.

I wandered through the hospital or nurses quarters and sat on the front steps, my twenty-six-year-old mind filled with thoughts and rumors.

We kept hearing reports on the advance of the Japanese army. They had reached the outskirts of Manila. Our soldiers destroyed everything useful that they couldn't take with them.

I carried with me a trifold slip that explained why I had been left behind—to furnish the Mactan—and described me as a noncombatant.

I tried to prepare myself to become a prisoner of war. I didn't know if God thought I could handle the stress of life as a prisoner. A prisoner of war!

Thoughts flooded my mind as I waited for the orders to board the Mactan, which Filipino students were painting white with red crosses to identify the inter-island steamer as a mercy ship. I wandered through the nurses' quarters and sat on the stairs at Sternberg Hospital. I wanted to be with the other nurses.

Retrieving photos from the club

TWO NAVY OFFICERS, whom I had met earlier when I dined aboard their submarine in Manila Bay, stopped by the hospital. They invited me to dinner. I imagined Colonel Carroll would have no objection, so I agreed.

I rode the mule during the Army-Navy game celebrations in November 1941, the month before war came to the Philippine Islands. Below is a photo of men on the stage. On my last visit to the Army-Navy Club, Captain Ruth and I saw photos from the previous month's festivities. He urged me to take the photos and when I hesitated, he said: "Do you want the Japs to have them?" I took the photos and carried them in my musette bag.

*Enjoying the Army-Navy game festivities above
are nurses Hattie Brantley and Minnie Breese,
Majors Tom Tarpley and Guy Stubbs, me and
Major Sam Lamb. Below is the stage where
performances took place.*

We drove in the dark through a very depressed city, brightened only by blasting and flames from the items being destroyed by the American forces. Believe it or not, we took time to eat a steak dinner. All the time the Irish-American officer carried on about how their submarine sustained eight hits and sat half-submerged in the bay. They had worked all day trying to salvage it, but with little success. After dinner we returned to the hospital—another few hours of reality in the very, very unreal.

In the days before the fall of Manila, Captain Ruth of the medical corps and three corpsmen had acquired a truck and drove it from Bataan to Manila to scrounge for all the medical supplies they could lay their hands on. When the captain saw me, he asked why I was still in Manila.

He added: "Do you realize how near the Japanese are? You should get out of here! "

"I cannot do that," I answered. "I have another assignment."

He accepted my answer, then asked: "Well, how about going to the Army-Navy Club for a drink?"

I said I would ask the medical doctor in charge. He was reluctant to let me go but Captain Ruth talked him into it.

When we arrived at the club we found it overflowing with military families who had refused to leave the Philippines when instructed to do so.

In the entrance hall we saw a bulletin board with four large pictures of the last Army-Navy football game. Lo and behold, one photograph showed me riding the Army mule. Dr. Ruth asked if I wanted the photos.

I hesitated, asking: "May I take them?"

He said: "Do you want the Japs to have them?"

"Of course not," I said, so he removed the photos from the board and gave them to me. I kept the pictures in my musette bag and brought them home to the States.

On December 31, 1941, as I continued to wait, a very upset lieutenant from Brooklyn who had been assigned to stay with me each day as a sort of guardian angel, I suppose, kept pacing back and forth. Every once in a while, he'd ask: "When are you leaving? Do you know how close they are? Do you know they're right outside the city?"

I said, "Yes, I know they're right outside the city."

With the Japanese less than ten kilometers away, he fretted since he couldn't leave for Bataan until our ship left Manila Bay.

Later in the afternoon, I said aloud: "You know, an ice cream cone would be just wonderful!" We had food available, yet I had found my desire to eat greatly lacking. But I loved ice cream—a favorite treat of mine anytime.

During this time, medical doctors went through the wards identifying soldiers too seriously injured to be moved and selecting those who could survive a month aboard the Mactan. Army soldiers being cared for at Santa Scholastica College by Navy nurses also received the option of traveling on the Mactan, the first hospital ship to carry wounded during World War II.

(Years later, at a reunion of the Defenders of Bataan and Corregidor, a man who discovered I had served as the nurse aboard the Mactan told me: "Ma'am, I always wanted to meet you. I was in the Navy that night the Mactan left. I was a patient at Sternberg. When they selected patients to sail on the Mactan, they asked me if I wanted to be transferred to the Navy hospital or to sail on the hospital ship. I did the dumbest thing in my life—I selected to be transferred to the Navy and I became a prisoner.")

Finally, at about 6 P.M. on New Year's Eve 1941, a military car pulled up before the hospital with Colonel Carroll sitting in the back seat.

"Come on. Get in," he said to me. "We are going."

I grabbed my small khaki musette bag, slipped into the car next to him and we started slowly moving forward. With my window rolled down, suddenly—lo and behold, miracle of miracles—I saw the anxious lieutenant jogging to keep pace with the car as he reached inside to hand me an ice cream cone!

Shortly before the Japanese arrived in Manila, I retrieved photos from the wall of the Army-Navy Club, pictured above. Below, alone at the Sternberg nurses' quarters, I carried a card identifying me as a noncombatant, in case the Japanese arrived before the Mactan sailed.

—Top photo courtesy of the
Battling Bastards of Bataan.

STERNBERG GENERAL HOSPITAL - MANILA, P.I.

The bearer, whose signature appears hereon, is a member of the Medical Corps of the U. S. Army, and is a non-combatant left for the care of the sick and wounded only.

FLORAMUND FELLMUTH, 2d Lt, ANC

P. J. CARROLL,
Colonel, Medical Corps, U.S.Army

I drove to the docks eating a vanilla ice cream cone. What a way to go!

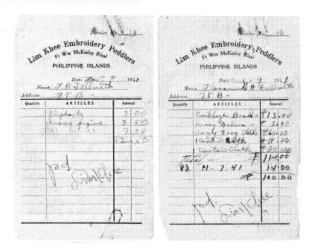

Although I left the Philippines under siege, I still received an invoice in January 1948 for $100 still owning on a dress I charged and wore to the Army-Navy game. I received the letter, left, and invoices, center, from Lim Khee Embroidery Peddlers. The bottom slips show I repaid the debt during the summer and fall.

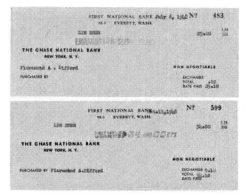

Chapter Six

Sailing Aboard the Mactan

Stormy Seas, Death and Uncertainty

Volunteers painted the Mactan white with a Red Cross to identify it as a mercy ship. Below, the Mactan left Pier Seven in Manila Bay before midnight December 31, 1941, with Captain Julian Tamayo at the helm.

Boarding the Mactan

WE ARRIVED AT THE LARGE STEEL and concrete Pier Seven, where ambulances, buses, taxis, Army trucks, jeeps and bread vans arrived with wounded men who were carried or hobbled up the narrow gangplank of the recently painted inter-island coconut husk steamer.

The 2,067-ton rusty steamer Mactan, built in 1899, had been dropping off guns, ammunition and clothing at Marivales at the tip of Bataan when the Red Cross asked her to return to Manila, according to Bill Noyer, author of the book *Mactan: Ship of Destiny*. The decrepit ship had served as an inter-island steamer, but nearly everyone doubted her seaworthiness in stormy ocean waters.

At the request of General Douglas MacArthur on December 28, the American Red Cross had agreed to charter the 300-foot-long oil-fired steamer from its owners, Compania Maritima, at a cost of $1,000 a day, Noyer stated. The Red Cross commissioned the ship in the name of the United States president.

Nearly a hundred university students had volunteered to paint the vessel white with red crosses on its sides and decks so planes could recognize the mercy ship from the sky. They also painted a red band nearly five feet wide around the vessel. Whining winches lifted boxes of supplies from the dock and deckhands guided them into the ship's hold, while other cranes dumped boxes of .30-caliber rifles used during World War I into the bay.

Altogether, 224 injured officers and enlisted men arrived at the docks, where orderlies carried them aboard the ship for an uncertain journey whose destination—Australia— remained a secret to most.

John Cook, a Texan who had served as a medic in the operating room at Fort McKinley, helped load the seriously wounded patients onto the Mactan under the covered Pier Seven in Manila. He was one of eight people serving as litter bearers. (I met him in May 2000 at a reunion of the Defenders of Bataan and Corregidor in Reno, Nevada, where he introduced himself to me and mentioned he had helped load patients onto the Mactan.)

The loading of patients began at 4 P.M. and ended three hours later. While Japanese planes circled the city, vehicles brought patients from both Sternberg hospital and Santa Scholastica, where Navy nurses were tending the wounded. I didn't learn until years later that three ambulances headed for Bataan were misdirected and those patients sailed aboard the Mactan.

Before I boarded the ship, a doctor—a lieutenant colonel—provided me with all the medications we'd need for the trip: morphine, barbiturates and other pain-relieving drugs. At the time, I wore men's khaki pants and a men's shirt. He said to me: "Well, you know, I guess you can button them in your pockets." Throughout the entire trip, I alone kept track of the medication given to patients and administered the meds to the patients day and night.

I didn't know anyone at the docks, so I walked up the gangplank to the ship, which was run by a Filipino crew under the supervision of Captain Julian Tamayo.

Altogether, the ship's medical crew included Colonel Percy Carroll as the chief surgeon and six Filipino doctors, one dentist and ten female and two male Filipino Red Cross nurses. I was the only Army nurse and the chief nurse.

Once aboard the ship, I met the Red Cross director, Irving Williams, who appeared busy overseeing the loading of patients, supplies and the crew. For days he had been supervising the ship's conversion from a freighter to a hospital ship.

Prior to our coming on board, Mr. Williams had selected fifteen tiny rooms for the staff. My room, mid-ship outside on the starboard side, was just large enough for a cot, sink and toilet, about six feet square in size. Outside my room, I took two steps down to reach the deck. In the other direction, a narrow gangway led to the engine room. To reach the hold, which was covered with dried coconut husk chips, you had to climb down straight steel ladders.

When I first met Father Shanahan aboard the Mactan, he wore a white cassock so I offered to let him wear some of my clothes—khaki pants and shirt. He said he'd never forget meeting me. I helped persuade him to join the Army as a chaplain.

Meeting Father Shanahan

RETURNING TO THE DECK where Irving Williams directed operations, I was seeing to it that patients were made comfortable when I looked up and saw a tall man in a priest's white tropical cassock standing before me.

He carried aboard the ship a small bag, which he laid down before handing me a letter from his superior. The

The Mactan left Manila from Pier Seven, pictured above. I am seen with Col. Percy J. Carroll on the deck from inside the Mactan. Below, four of the Mactan's patients are seen on the ship's deck.

letter, written to Thomas J. Wolff, chairman of the Philippine Red Cross, introduced the Reverend Thomas A. Shanahan of Waterbury, Connecticut, S.J., an English professor at the Jesuit University, Ateneo de Manila, and the Mactan's chaplain.

"And I take it that you're Father Shanahan?" I asked him.

He told me he had been at Red Cross headquarters and overheard Colonel Carroll, Mr. Wolff and Mr. Forster talking about a Red Cross hospital ship. When he asked if they needed a chaplain, Colonel Carroll said, 'Sure, come on along.'

Father Shanahan looked around the deck and asked, "Where should I place my things?"

I took him below and found him a small stateroom. He set down his luggage and asked, "What may I do to help?"

"We need someone to hurry the unloading of the cargo," I answered, hesitating as I looked at him in his long white robe. "Well, it'll never do in what you're wearing. I'll go get you a set of my clothes."

His startled expression was worth a thousand words!

He said, "You'll do what?"

"I'll give you an outfit," I told him. Then he realized I was wearing a soldier's shirt and pants. I gave him the extra pair of men's Army khakis that I had been issued. They fit him.

When Father came out dressed in tans, I said, "Follow me." I led him to where the Mactan's previous cargo of guns and ammunition was being dumped overboard. I asked him to see what he could do to help.

Later he said he'd never forget his introduction to me.

Patients on the decks

I RETURNED TO THE DECK and saw injured men lying on Army cots, straw mattresses or wooden pallets doing duty as makeshift hospital beds—with others on mattress-

American and Filipino patients aboard the Mactan relax on cots beneath canvas coverings.

es on the upper aft deck. Some lay on the canvas stretchers on which they'd been carried aboard.

Some men had arms or legs in casts; others wore bandages covering their heads and faces. Many had been wounded in the twenty-three days since war had come to the Philippine Islands December 8.

It took until after dark for men to unload the Mactan's old cargo and finish bringing aboard patients and supplies. Floodlights shone on the red crosses of the brightly painted white ship to let the Japanese know this was a mercy ship.

I tried to make the patients as comfortable as possible.

One of the patients, Private Edward E. Mosier of Deer Lodge, Montana, suffered shock when a bomber struck nearby officers' quarters Dec. 8. I helped him as he came up the gangplank and reassured him that we were going to try to make it to Australia, which made him feel better.

Among the last of the wounded to come aboard, about seven o'clock, was Captain William A. Fairfield, who was unable to move as a full body plaster cast covered him from under his armpits down to his ankles. I remember I questioned him. He said his leg had started hurting.

"I'll take care of you," I said. By that time, I'd made a quick scan of the boat. I said: "I'll have you moved down below to one of the rooms inside."

Father Shanahan came along about the same time and asked Captain Fairfield how he was doing and introduced himself as the chaplain.

Orderlies carried Captain Fairfield below and strapped him to the bunk in a small stateroom outside of what had been the dining room, which we converted into an operating room. He shared the tiny stateroom with Second Lieutenant Bartholomeo Passanante of Philadelphia, who was placed on a stack of mattresses on the floor. The small stateroom also contained a window.

Awaiting Japanese clearance

Red Cross officials had sent a radio message to Tokyo seeking permission for the Mactan to leave Manila and sail to Australia. The Swiss Consul in Manila inspected the ship about 7:30 P.M. to ascertain it carried no contraband and served only as a hospital ship carrying wounded, as outlined by the Second Geneva Convention terms in 1906.

However, Japan had never signed that treaty and never responded to say whether the Mactan would be guaranteed safe passage to Australia.

No one knew whether the ship would be destroyed by the Japanese and sunk in the bay or the open seas. This was the first hospital ship scheduled to transport American casualties in a war that the United States had only just entered.

The captain didn't have any detailed maps of the dangerous reefs in the seas to the south. The maps had been destroyed when the Japanese bombed the United States Coast and Geodetic Survey office. Another ship—the Don Esteban from Corregidor—agreed to rendezvous with the

The Science

To be
 a nurse
  is to be
   peaceful
    enough
with yourself
 to leave
  yourself
   and enter
within
 the life
  of another...

A poem by Wynona Bice-Stephens from her book, *The Art of Nursing*

Mactan off the breakwater about 11 P.M. to bring more comprehensive maps, according to Noyer.

So without detailed maps and without Japanese clearance, the Mactan weighed anchor and started its engines about 8:30 P.M., maneuvering its way through the watery grave-yard of Manila Bay, where the Japanese had sunk many a ship during the previous three weeks.

John Cook and the others who had loaded patients sat on the dock watching as the Mactan made its way out of Manila Bay. They had thought they'd be leaving on the Mactan with the patients they'd carried aboard, he told oral history interviewer Katherine Clark in November 1997.

But instead, he recalled that they felt abandoned as they watched the Mactan sail away before they boarded a lumber freighter—the Don Juan—for a twenty-mile trip to Bataan. Japanese planes laid down strafing fire and dropped bombs but missed the freighter. He became a prisoner of war for thirty-four months.

Manila burning

WHILE WAITING TO RENDEZVOUS with the Don Esteban, a small group of us gathered on the bridge for a last look at Manila's skyline. I stood there with Irving Williams, Colonel Carroll, Father Shanahan and the skipper, Captain Julian C. Tamayo.

Bright flames hung over Manila, which had been declared an open city, as retreating American troops dynamited gasoline storage tanks and destroyed anything they thought Japanese soldiers might use.

At midnight, just off Corregidor, I remember watching the flames in Manila and hearing the sheet music my sister Colette had bought called, "The Burning of Rome." It looked like the picture on the front of the sheet music.

What a way to greet the New Year, 1942. Williams offered cigars to the men.

"Happy New Year," Father Shanahan said. Noyer wrote

that the priest then left to join some of the other nurses
and patients, where he led them in prayer and said: "Our
destiny is in God's hands."

Zigzag through a minefield

ALTHOUGH THE DON ESTEBAN met the Mactan just
before midnight, Captain Tamayo discovered the
charts brought to him were too general, not the more spe-
cific ones he'd requested. He worried about how the ship
would weather rough water and tropical storms on the
open seas.

He also needed to guide the ship in the darkness through
the minefields that guarded the entrance to Manila Bay.
Only a few weeks earlier, on December 16, a faster inter-
island steamer, the SS Corregidor, had hit a mine in the
dark channel and sank quickly, killing 400 people while
280 survived, Noyer wrote.

Unlike the skipper of the Corregidor, the Mactan's captain
waited for guidance from the Navy's Inshore Patrol, which
sent a small corvette from Corregidor to guide the ship
through the maze of mines on the one and only zigzag
route that offered safe passage to the sea.

I stood at the railing beside Father Shanahan, watching
the drama unfold. We did not realize the slow lumbering
Mactan following the gray corvette had made a wrong turn
in the dark until a Navy sailor bellowed into a megaphone
in a deep monotone: "Keep to the right! Keep to the
right!"

According to George Korson in his book, *At His Side: The
American Red Cross Overseas in World War II*, the fellow
aboard the corvette yelled: "You damn fools! Do you want
to blow yourselves to kingdom come? Follow instructions!"

Finally, after making one sharp turn after another, the
corvette signaled farewell and good luck, and then headed
back to Corregidor.

Without detailed maps, the small and lonely old Mactan
was headed into the South China Sea for Australia at a

maximum cruising speed of thirteen knots.

I turned to the passengers, many of them needing pain medication. Passengers and crew worried about their fate and that of the small ship, which could be bombed by the Japanese, capsized in heavy seas, ripped apart on a ragged reef, or maybe—with a miracle—make it to Australia.

The first day out

AFTER LEAVING MANILA BEHIND in a blaze, we made the patients as comfortable as possible and tried to sleep, despite not knowing whether we'd survive the 5,000-mile journey to Australia.

On that Thursday morning, January 1, 1942, while the Japanese continued firing at American and Filipino forces in the Philippines, the Mactan sailed in the South China Sea, heading for Darwin, Australia, normally a ten-day journey. The old steamer carried 316 people: 224 patients, a crew of sixty-seven and twenty-five medical and Red Cross staff.

That first day out, Colonel Carroll assigned the six Filipino doctors to different sections of the ship and I assigned the Red Cross nurses and orderlies to their duties, locations and twelve-hour shifts.

I didn't have a section myself: I saw every patient throughout the day during formal rounds, as did Colonel Carroll. I also dispensed all the painkillers and other medications—day or night. We had to prepare morphine the old-fashioned way, boiling water and putting the morphine into a spoon.

The first morning, when the Filipino crew prepared breakfast of scrambled eggs, sausage and bread, they worried because they couldn't find the coffee pitchers normally on board. The nurses told them what had happened: some of the men used the pitchers as urinals during the night and tossed them overboard into the sea.

Food—the lack of it and the lack of variety—became an irritant to the wounded on board, many of whom lost

Three of the men instrumental in caring for patients aboard the Mactan were Colonel Carroll, left, Father Shanahan, center, and Irving Williams, the Red Cross director.

weight and complained about the food throughout the trip, according to Noyer, author of the book *Mactan.* I think one of the problems proved to be the food appealed to the Filipino diet, but didn't tempt the palates of American wounded.

Without enough plates and silverware for everyone, the wounded ate in shifts, with patients who could move helping to serve those who were bedridden. The crew washed the dishes in boiling saltwater before serving the second shift.

As we sailed on, Father Shanahan maneuvered packing crates into place to create a makeshift altar. He donned his white clerical robes and celebrated Mass. The rest of the day, he did whatever he could to help the rest of us.

The patients, crowded on the decks in cots or on mattresses, were crammed together under a canvas covering to protect the men from the heat of the tropical sun or the pelting rain if storms occurred. We did formal rounds twice a day, assessing the wounds of each man and comparing what we saw to the sparse medical records we brought with us.

We also determined that, to preserve the ship's limited supply of fresh water, all bathing and washing would need to be done in seawater, or brine.

Then I went below to the dining area, which contained cabinets for china and silver. I assigned a Red Cross nurse who had served aboard a ship in the past to set up the operating room. We had a portable operating table brought aboard and placed in the dining area, where the light cast by electric lamps left a lot to be desired.

The next day, after passing through the Mindoro Strait into the Sulu Sea, Colonel Carroll and Mr. Williams, along with a member of the ship's crew, started organizing lifeboat drills so patients would know what to do in case of an emergency. The ship had only six lifeboats but fifteen life rafts and many life preservers.

We had determined that the men in the casts could be dropped overboard wearing two life preservers and the plaster cast would disintegrate in the water. Then they would be pulled aboard lifeboats.

Dining aboard the ship

THE DINING ARRANGEMENTS called for me to eat with Mr. Williams, Colonel Carroll and Father Shanahan. We enjoyed each other's company, getting to know one another during a very tense voyage. The Red Cross doctors and nurses ate together outside on a raised deck covered by canvas.

Father Shanahan, who came from Waterbury, Connecticut, had been a professor at the seminary in Manila. He was a great consolation to everyone. Toward the end of the voyage we had convinced him to join the Army.

Irving Williams always took care of himself. And since we dined with him, we also shared in his meals, which sometimes included food that didn't wind up on the plates of the patients. As the man in charge of the Red Cross ship, I suppose he might have felt pretty important.

The three of them—Williams, Colonel Carroll and Father Shanahan—took great delight in kidding me about one thing or another. We developed a kind of camaraderie.

But those supplying the Filipino crew bought the food for the patients, too, so they brought rice and other staples of the Filipino diet. Mr. Williams brought aboard special things, and we shared that food, but I didn't have any great desire to eat. We had food, but we had so much going on that eating barely crossed the mind. You ate and returned to your duties right away.

That night, January 2, when the ship maneuvered off the northeast coast of Borneo in the Sulu Sea, the captain realized the winds were blowing the Mactan toward the treacherous Pearl Reef, named for a pearl farm at Marungas Island. Captain Tamayo wanted to navigate the dangerous reef during daylight hours, but he also worried about being spotted by the Japanese stationed at Davao on the island of Mindanao and in northeastern Borneo, according to Korson in *At His Side*.

The captain decided the coral reef posed the greatest danger, so he slowed the ship to seven knots, then circled back and backtracked through the night for five hours until the sun rose, when he turned back on course to pass the coral reefs in daylight hours.

During the night, the seas calmed and the sky cleared for a couple of hours, so moonlight lit the path of the Mactan, which remained illuminated at all times in accordance with international law regarding hospital ships. Then clouds returned, the seas grew rough and a light rain fell.

The storm and changing course made many of the patients, nurses, doctors and even the crew nauseous. The nurses bathed the patients and cared for them, but when the seas grew rough, many of the young nurses became very sick, which doubled the workload of those who didn't succumb to seasickness.

Patients battle ants, Manila falls

THE NEXT MORNING, Saturday, January 3, as we made our rounds of the patients, several asked Father Shanahan and Mr. Williams—who distributed cigarettes and magazines among the men—why we'd changed course during the night. At first Williams denied that the ship changed course, stating instead that we simply were ahead of schedule. According to Korson, when a B-17 navigator asked why the moon was on the wrong side of the ship, Williams finally confessed to the backtracking done so the Mactan could maneuver past the reef in daylight.

The rough seas in the early morning hours posed a problem for the patients on the decks. To keep them from being soaked, the crew covered their cots and mattresses with large canvasses.

It didn't take long before the patients started complaining about intense itching and pain.

When we pulled back their bandages to examine their festering wounds, we found their bodies crawling with little red ants. Some of the little insects had crawled inside the men's plaster casts, causing intense itching that they couldn't scratch.

The ship, which had been used as a freighter hauling coconut husks, crawled with cockroaches, little red ants and copra beetles, or copra bugs, which fed on the dried nutritive tissue of coconuts—the copra.

The orderlies filled cans with water and placed the legs of each cot in the cans so the ants couldn't crawl onto the patients. We changed the bandages and sprayed inside casts with handheld sprayers. Fortunately we had the sprayers on board.

Father Shanahan took a crew of men to scrub the ship from top to bottom.

The third day brought us news over the radio of a very sad event—the fall of Manila.

After supper one of the crew with a short-wave radio in his

cabin heard a radio report from San Francisco, which interrupted a musical broadcast:

"Repeating the announcement made over this station earlier today—the city of Manila was occupied by Japanese troops at ten o'clock this morning. The Japanese were at the gates of the city yesterday, but delayed entry until they could organize a triumphal march into the ancient capital of the Philippines."

The news reverberated like a shockwave through the ship since many of the wounded Filipino soldiers and the Red Cross doctors and nurses had left family members behind.

One of the nurses, Elisa N. Domingo, left four children with her mother when she boarded the Mactan. According to Korson, author of *At His Side*, she wailed: "My children, my babies! Why did I leave them?"

Captain Julian Tamayo had left behind his wife and five children. As tears streamed down faces, Father Shanahan did his best to calm everyone, asking them to place their faith in their Savior and "dedicate yourselves before Christ, to do your utmost to restore your country to your people..."

Later that night, Father Shanahan visited Williams in his cabin. Williams had thought they would have time for another trip back to the Philippines for more wounded.

According to Korson, Father Shanahan, puffing on his pipe, reminisced with Williams about his years as a Jesuit missionary and teacher among the Filipinos, whom he described as "a devout, decent, sturdy little people."

Father waits for Floramund

THE NEXT MORNING, January 4, the sun shone in a clear tropical sky while the Mactan steamed through the Celebes Sea toward the Makassar Straits. Father Shanahan planned to hold Sunday Mass beginning at 9 A.M., using an improvised altar.

I was still seeing to my nursing duties with the patients when nine o'clock approached, so Father Shanahan sent a messenger to remind me about the Mass.

I told the messenger, "And would you go back and tell Father that I'm busy?"

He sent back another message saying: "Just let me know when you can get here." So I hurried and he told everyone he had to wait till I arrived—and he did. So I said, "This is the first time in my life I ever pulled rank on God!" No one seemed to mind the delay because, after all, we weren't going anywhere.

I tried to attend Mass every day, and if I couldn't make it—if I were giving medicines or caring for a patient—Father Shanahan always waited for me.

We crossed the equator at noon and Captain Tamayo blew the ship's whistle in acknowledgement of the occasion. "The Captain insisted on paying his respects to old Father Neptune," Captain Fairfield wrote in his diary. Fairfield, who retired as a major from the U.S. Air Corps, kept the diary from the first week of December 1941 through January 1942.

Captain Fairfield and a seriously injured patient, Lieutenant Passanante, shared the same small stateroom during the voyage. The staff found it simpler that way to take care of their severe pain and to provide simple meals, such as beef broth and rice, which was the only food they could tolerate. To prepare morphine for patients, I had to use a spoon, boiling water and measuring drops. Today, the medicines are sent from the pharmacy completely prepared, but that wasn't the case in 1941.

Captain Tamayo, who frequently puffed on cigars, told Red Cross director Williams that the Mactan was low on oil and water, in large part because it carried so many more passengers than usual. While worried about changing course, which might give Japanese fighters an excuse to attack, Tamayo also knew he had to have oil and water. So he and Williams decided to stop at Makassar in the Netherlands East Indies, at the southwestern tip of Celebes Island.

After contacting the American consul by radio and determining within two hours that it wasn't a Japanese ruse, the

Colonel Percy J. Carroll served as the Mactan's chief surgeon and only
Army doctor, while I served as the chief nurse and only Army nurse. We
are seen at the bow of the Mactan.

Dutch naval commander agreed to send a pilot boat to
help the Mactan navigate the reefs around the island.

Traumatic surgery aboard ship

AS THE MACTAN MADE its way through stormy waters
under gray rainy skies that Monday, January 5,
patients and nurses alike suffered seasickness.

One of the Americans tried to rouse a Filipino soldier who
had been seasick since leaving Manila. The critically
injured patient, who never should have been brought
aboard the Mactan, lay curled on deck with a blanket over
his face. When the American shook his shoulder, the man
didn't speak or move. He had died—our first great loss.

As mountainous waves struck the ship, lurching it side-
ways and skidding the cots across the deck, cross winds
flapped the canvas coverings designed to keep the rain
from drenching patients' beds. Nurses had to change
linens on the wet beds on the rocking, swaying ship while
orderlies pulled cots back from the rails. The waves
drenched nurses, doctors and patients who tried to escape
the torrent.

After leaving Manila, the Mactan received permission to dock at Makassar to bury two soldiers who had died during the early part of the journey. Medical staff and patients who could walk left the ship while it was in the Dutch East Indies.

In the makeshift operating room, the former dining salon, the tumultuous rocking and lurching of the ship tossed bottles, dressings and other items onto the floor.

During the height of the storm, one of the patients who suffered from wounds in his arm and shoulder began hemorrhaging. The doctor in charge started a plasma transfusion immediately and tried to stop the bleeding with gauze.

I remember going down to ask the Filipino nurse, whom I had assigned to set up the surgery, where I could find the sterile surgical gloves. However, she was the first one to become deathly ill. She lay on her cot moaning with seasickness.

In response to my question, she rolled her head toward me and said, "Gloves, mum?" She was so very ill.

So I looked at one of the doctors and said, "Would you follow me, please? How do you get to the bottom of this ship?"

He showed me where to find the iron ladder leading downward, so the two of us climbed down into the hull, where we found a deck of coconut husks. The boxes had been dumped atop the coconut husks. I just looked at the boxes and I said to him: "Open that box." He picked up a tool, pried open the lid and at the very top sat the sterile gloves. I felt grateful for yet another "knowing."

We rushed back to the operating room, accompanied by Miriam Fowles, a Canadian-born nurse married to an English diplomat, and Basilia Hernando, the senior Filipino nurse. The three of us proceeded to set up the operating room.

Because of the ship's tossing, the crew and staff had banked cases of canned goods around the base of the portable operating table to keep it from moving.

Colonel Carroll, who had been called by the time we had set up the operating room, realized immediately he would need to operate on the soldier's arm.

The ship continued to lurch, pitch and roll forcing Colonel Carroll to try to keep his footing while deftly working at lightening speed to stop the loss of blood. Then the lights failed, making a tense situation even worse. I beckoned to Irving Williams, who was watching the operation, indicating we needed a flashlight. Someone aimed the flashlight at the surgical table, where Colonel Carroll leaned over the patient and listened. We had lost our second patient.

I moved to the colonel quickly and untied his mask. He didn't say a word, simply left the room while others moved around the table where the patient lay.

I spread my hands in a gesture of despair. Walking toward Williams, I murmured simply: "Thrombosis." A blood clot had formed in a blood vessel; the clot blocked an artery to the heart.

Later in the day, after the case was over, the doctor who had helped me find the surgical gloves came to me and said: "Ma'am, any time you want anything done, just let me know. I'd follow you wherever you want. I'd follow you."

In the afternoon, about two o'clock, a pilot boat arrived to guide the Mactan to the Dutch Indies, which resembled a fishing port in Holland, although this port was in the South Seas. When the Mactan pulled alongside one of the two long concrete landing piers, officials from the city that 3,500 Europeans called home boarded our ship.

We received permission to bury at Makassar the two soldiers who had died, which saved us from having to bury them at sea. I also spoke with the major doctor and Mr. Williams about medical supplies we would need. We obtained other supplies for the ship, in addition to oil and water, such as clean linens, food and navigational charts.

We remained at Makassar for a few days, trying to ascertain the ship's final destination from people at Darwin and the American Legation at Canberra in Australia. The first words from the Americans were: "Are you all right? There's a report that you'd been bombed."

Newspapers in Australia and the United States erroneously reported that the Japanese had attacked the Mactan. What we heard made us worry that the false accusations could incite the Japanese to make those reports accurate by truly attacking our white mercy ship with its large red cross, above which flew both the United States and Red Cross flags.

Burying two soldiers at Makassar

ABOUT MID-MORNING on Tuesday, January 6, Father Shanahan, Colonel Carroll, Irving Williams and I climbed into a taxi at the dock. We rode with the windows open because we found the heat inside the cab quite muggy and suffocating.

At the cemetery, we saw two rough wooden caskets lying beside the open graves. These were our Filipino patients, the two who didn't survive the early part of our journey.

They would be laid to rest at Makassar, given full military rites by a small company of Dutch soldiers and a drum and bugle corps.

Rites for Two of Gen. MacArthur's Forces
Father Shanahan, chaplain of the Mactan, reads the burial service for two soldiers who died during the trip from Manila to Makassar. The ship carried 300 wounded American and Filipino soldiers of Gen. MacArthur's forces from Manila to Australia.

At Makassar, Colonel Carroll, Irving Williams, Father Shanahan and I attended the last rites for two patients who died during the Mactan's journey. Below, the two coffins were constructed on the deck of the Mactan.

As the blazing sun beat down on our group gathered at the gravesides, we sweltered wearing military uniforms in the tropical heat.

Father Shanahan read the burial service for the two Filipino soldiers—Corporal Salvador Dayem and Private Lucio Pequilla.

When we returned to the ship, we found that a number of ambulatory patients had left the ship to stretch their legs.

As the ship remained docked at Makassar, I ventured ashore, only to discover that the streets seemed deserted except for a few natives carrying guns, shovels and picks and a handful of public officials. Most of the residents had been evacuated as the island prepared for Japanese attacks. We dined at the home of one of the Dutch officials at Makassar.

The weather remained hot and sunny.

One morning, an air raid siren suddenly blared, piercing the tropical quiet and causing panic among the Mactan's wounded. By February 12, the Rising Sun flag would be flying on the island.

The air raid drill upset Colonel Carroll, who described it as the last straw. He felt the wounded men needed proper hospital care, which they couldn't obtain on the ship.

Leaving Makassar

FINALLY, THE MACTAN with her anxious patients and Red Cross staff received the go-ahead to leave Makassar on Thursday, January 8, heading for Australia. Williams had been instructed to sail to the first port on the east coast of Australia, which would be Townsville—a ten-day journey from Makassar past Thursday Island.

Officials at Darwin recommended taking the ship to Brisbane, but Williams thought Darwin offered the best hope, so he asked if the ship could proceed there. He didn't receive any response from the British naval minister in Canberra.

As the ship left Makassar, the Dutch Navy provided

instructions on which way to go. Fortunately, the Mactan took a different route, rather than following the instructions provided by the German consulate, who remained at Makassar with his wife. Had we followed his instructions, the Mactan would have sailed directly into the Japanese landing forces.

The ship left Makassar during the evening of Friday, January 9, sailing through storms and heat while the patients, staff and crew continually worried over an imminent Japanese attack. Workers draped a new tarpaulin along the back deck to shelter patients from the sun.

According to Noyer, Williams spent $2,000 in Makassar on supplies, including oil, water, tins of Dutch chocolate, bananas, beef, rope, brushes, underwear, cigarettes, postcards, coal and a thousand pounds of ice for refrigeration.

On Saturday, January 10, we sailed through the Flores Sea under a blazing sun but calm waters. Father Shanahan moved from one bed to another, visiting with patients and asking the names of relatives to notify of their safety once they reached Darwin.

He spoke in English and then in Tagalog, but at one bed, the man merely shrugged and shook his head, according to the book by Noyer. His right hand had been amputated at the wrist. He didn't understand either language but may have understood one of the eighty dialects spoken in the Philippines. One of the other Filipinos identified him as Estanislas Osias, nineteen, and said he sits all day staring at the water.

Ship trailed by plane

AT ONE POINT AFTER LEAVING the Dutch East Indies, we spied a plane close to shore, paralleling the Mactan's course.

We watched the dark-colored plane, anxiously wondering whether it could be a Japanese bomber intending to attack the mercy ship. We couldn't hide anywhere; we simply continued plowing through the seas heading for Darwin.

We did not know what kind of plane it was; we never saw

Injured soldiers are seen lying or sitting on cots on the back deck of the Mactan.

it up close. We couldn't even tell if it was a Japanese plane; we didn't see any insignias.

We all worried that perhaps the plane would change course and drop bombs to sink the ship full of wounded soldiers and medical workers.

We had heard that the United States believed the Mactan had been sunk in a Japanese attack, and many newspapers erroneously reported the attack as fact. We anticipated an attack, but it never happened.

The ship continued through the Suva Sea but since Captain Tamayo didn't want to arrive at Darwin in the dark of night, he dropped anchor in a cove near Timor Island at 11 A.M. that Sunday, January 11, about thirty-six hours away from the town.

Father Shanahan, a twinkle in his eye, asked me: "How's your schedule this morning? Will you be able to come to services?"

Remembering the previous Sunday, when the priest delayed services until I arrived, I replied: "Why yes, of course."

Then he sent a messenger around to tell everyone we could have services.

Everyone enjoyed Father Shanahan, whose strong faith and wonderful sense of humor proved a consolation to the men and the staff. Colonel Carroll and I talked to him many times about joining the Army when we reached Australia. We knew he would make a great chaplain.

During the night, the ship left the Timor Sea and sailed toward Darwin.

The men aboard the ship spent time playing solitaire, chess, checkers and cribbage. Others wrote in diaries or letters home.

Docking at Darwin

IN THE MORNING of January 13, an Australian gunboat escorted the Mactan into the harbor at Darwin, where we received a loud welcome of horns, whistles and cheers from Allied ships in the harbor.

Darwin officials said they'd been told the ship had been bombed and sunk en route to Australia. Williams sent a note to the Red Cross in Washington, D.C., stating: "Unmolested en route."

Fearing Japanese attacks at Darwin, the Australians recommended that the Mactan continue its voyage farther along the coastline to Sydney.

Visitors arrived all that day and the next. Launches brought supplies from the Australian Red Cross and the military to the ship, including towels, chocolate, loaves of fresh bread, cookies and truckloads of ice for refrigeration. We also received medical supplies, Red Cross comfort items such as cigarettes, and a lieutenant from the USS Holland, which did the Mactan's laundry, brought aboard two American flags.

We were told we could pick up additional supplies at Townsville and Brisbane. Although they considered transferring patients to a bigger ship, the Manunda, officials felt the delay of a few days might prove too risky.

Beds lined the decks of the hospital ship, leaving only enough room for nurses and doctors to walk through to check on the patients.

During the day off Darwin, we were told that five Navy nurses aboard a launch could assist the Mactan during its journey. They had been headed to the Philippines before the war broke out, so their ship diverted to Australia. The ranking officers on the ship contacted Colonel Carroll to ask if he could transfer the nurses to the Mactan.

We needed help but I wasn't informed or consulted about any of the discussion until the launch arrived with five Navy nurses aboard. When two nurses boarded the ship, I received an introduction to the Navy officer and the nurses in their white uniforms. They explained the situation, saying the nurses could help on the ship. For a few minutes it sounded great, until the ranking nurse told us: "We do not perform bedside nursing." They supervised orderlies and others, distributed medicine and oversaw patients, but they didn't do hands-on bedside nursing.

When I heard that statement, I asked Colonel Carroll to step away a moment. I asked him to thank them but refuse because we needed nurses who would do bedside nursing. He agreed, thanking the nurses for their offer but turning it down. When I had time to think about it, I realized we didn't have billeting space for additional nurses.

The history of the Navy nurses in the Philippine Islands has been recorded in many other books.

Fire aboard the Mactan

THE MACTAN LEFT DARWIN at about 7 A.M. Thursday, January 15, on its way to Townsville, the next stop on the trip to Sydney. Patients watched from the rail as Darwin slipped away in the distance, then the Mactan sailed through Clarence Strait, across Van Diemen Gulf and through Dundas Strait, then east into Arafura Sea.

Then, shortly before 7 P.M., nurse Basilia Hernando shouted "Fire" while waving her arms toward black smoke billowing from a gangway that led to the engine room. Next we heard a dull explosion, followed by more smoke and flames. Alarms sounded and whistles blew as nurses and orderlies scrambled to prepare patients for emergency evacuation into the sea.

Colonel Carroll grabbed a fire extinguisher and rushed toward the engine room, but the heavy smoke forced him to retreat, gasping with a handkerchief over his face. He tried again with a Filipino patient, Private Lorenzo Gamboa, who took the fire extinguisher and forged ahead through the smoke, spraying to control the fire until the ship's crew came with hoses. (Note: The book, *At His Side*, and a newspaper article from the 1940s identified the patient as Jose Senorosa, but Noyer identified him as Lorenzo Gamboa.)

At the same time, Captain Tamayo pointed the ship toward the distant shore.

The patients put on their life preservers, and Father Shanahan, orderlies and nurses helped those patients who needed help getting into the preservers. Patients with casts received a second life jacket to use if they found themselves in the water to buoy the plaster casts until the water soaked them off. Lifeboat attendants stood ready to drop the boats into the water.

When I saw ambulatory patients jamming the deck and rushing forward to see the fire, I immediately anticipated a problem. I rushed to the upper deck where the ninety less-ill patients slept on mattresses. I instructed a sergeant (the same patient in the leg cast I'd cared for at Fort McKinley) to keep all the patients topside.

I worried that if all the patients scurried to one side of the ship, the extra weight could unbalance the Mactan and capsize her.

Immediately my mind flooded with memories of a great Chicago tragedy—the capsizing of the steamer Eastland on Lake Michigan July 24, 1915. Loaded with 2,400 people bound for a Western Electric Company picnic, the top-heavy excursion vessel suddenly capsized, perhaps from a sudden shift of passengers from one side to the other. Every Chicago neighborhood lost people when the Eastland capsized, claiming the lives of 835 people, mostly women and children.

Father Shanahan took charge of one side of the upper deck and I the other.

While fire raged, one patient broke the tension: "I have but one life to give. Period!" Then jokes started, averting panic. We were all grateful for that sense of humor, which softened each blow and helped us survive.

At 7:30 P.M., the all clear sounded. While only thirty minutes had passed—a relatively short time—it seemed an eternity while it lasted.

Safe again, the men burst into song.

As for the fire, it turned out that one of the fittings on the engine's pressure injector hadn't been tightened securely, which allowed oil to drip, causing a fire that spread flaming oil over the engine room's steel floor plate, according to Noyer. To quell the blaze, the ship's engineer had to turn off the fuel oil pump, which cut electricity, leaving the ship temporarily in darkness. The crew replaced the defective burner and restarted the fuel oil pump so the engine didn't stall.

Captain Tamayo commended Private Gamboa, who bravely battled the fire and emerged black from head to foot and slightly scalded by the live steam. Tamayo said the

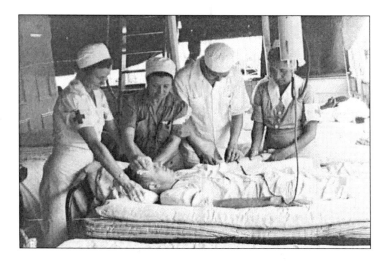

*Red Cross nurses, from left,
Katherine Owery, Miriam Fowles
and Basilia Hernando care for a
patient aboard the Mactan. The
doctor is unidentified.*

soldier's quick actions saved many lives as well as the
ship.

Settling into a shipboard routine

O N FRIDAY, JANUARY 16, yet another hot and humid
day, the ship's crew repaired damage to the engine
room caused by the fire.

As I made the rounds, I came upon a patient with malaria
who was freezing in the heat of the day. With blankets
piled on him, he recited a list of complaints to me, including his disgust with the "rotten" food.

Looking at him with no trace of a smile, I responded: "If
you don't like the service on board, you might try the
hotel across the street."

One look at the vast ocean surrounding the Mactan and he
decided to keep his complaints to himself.

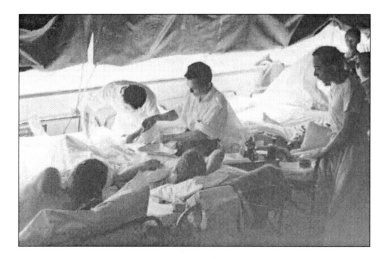

Doctors and nurses did their best to
care for patients during the journey
aboard the Mactan.

The next day, the Mactan crossed the northern tip of
Australia in calm seas under a clear but humid sky.

On January 18, Father Shanahan once again performed
Sunday services at his makeshift altar on the deck. As we
passed five miles from Thursday Island, a launch came
alongside the Mactan. Two captains boarded the ship to
guide her through the Great Barrier Reef and along the
Australian mainland to Brisbane.

I found it exciting when we passed Thursday Island
because I immediately thought of Mutiny on the Bounty.

During the day, the ship's radio announcer came on the
deck and breathlessly reported: "The Japanese announced
that they bombed the SS Mactan, a Red Cross hospital
ship."

We felt frightened then because we worried that perhaps
they still planned to bomb the ship, or at least that may
have been in their plans.

On Monday, January 19, the pilots navigated the Mactan
through the Torres Straits that separate Australia and New
Guinea.

As the patients continued complaining about the food, I decided to see what I could do to help. I went down below and spoke with Ramon Diaz, the chief steward.

"What can you do to make the meals more interesting?" I asked.

He rummaged through the pantry and the cooler, where I saw long salami sausages hanging.

"Let me see, we have some salami," he said.

"Well, slice it and get it out for lunch!"

The salami proved a welcome change in diet, but the complaints stemmed more from the traditional Filipino fare and lack of taste than from a shortage of food. The Filipinos didn't see any food shortage; they were happy eating rice, salted fish and peanuts. But the American soldiers weren't used to such meals, day after day, and they may have required more portions or more variety.

The next day, the Mactan continued its journey along the more mountainous Australian coastline toward Townsville, a small community where we could find supplies and clean linen.

A pilot came aboard the ship that night to guide her to the dock, where Australian Naval commanders had arranged for oil, water, laundry and other supplies for the ship.

Hello Townsville and Brisbane

WE ANCHORED IN TOWNSVILLE, a small city that reminded me of pictures of our American west in the old days.

The ladies of the Townsville Red Cross gave me a full supply of very bright printed cotton pajamas, which I promptly stored away to use when we arrived at our last stop, Sydney. They also brought aboard glasses, cups, bedspreads and books.

"This is the least we can offer in the face of the contribution the United States is making to our security," Mrs. W.J. Heatley, president of the Townsville Red Cross, is quoted as saying in Korson's book, *At His Side.*

Irving Williams and Colonel Carroll went ashore and bought milk, chocolate and ice cream.

Captain Fairfield wrote that the third engineer brought in supplies, including seven sacks of cement. When we asked what he would do with them, he told Fairfield to "just wait and see." Later, they learned he used the cement to bolster the inside of the ship to keep it from leaking and falling apart before reaching Sydney.

The ship left dock and headed out to sea again before 10:30 that night.

The weather continued rainy and stormy, with rough seas and cooler nights. The ship traveled past islands in the afternoon, where the passengers saw evergreens for the first time and villagers waving at the ship from the shore.

At 3 P.M. Saturday, January 24, the ship arrived at the mouth of the Brisbane River, eight miles from the city of Brisbane. As the ship made its way up the river, the citizens of Brisbane stood along hillsides above the river's shore, welcoming us with cheers and waving flags, bed sheets, tablecloths and handkerchiefs as we passed.

We learned that the first U.S. troops, initially bound for the Philippines, had arrived in Brisbane.

The staff was invited to the home of the American consul, Joseph P. Ragland, who suggested that everyone should inventory what they'd left behind in the Philippines for future claims. Although I wore soldier's khaki pants and shirts during most of the voyage, I had a few white duty uniforms that I donned when we docked at different ports.

A colonel arranged for delivery of the passengers' mail and Christmas packages, which had been sent to the men in the Philippines but was rerouted to Brisbane after the war began.

The Filipino crew found people they knew aboard the Don Isidro, a sister ship of the Don Esteban owned by Compania Maritima.

The men received a great treat—ice cream and milk!

Stormy seas and man overboard

LIEUTENANT ROBERT H. ODELL, assistant military attaché to the U.S. legation at Canberra, boarded the ship and went on with us to Sydney.

The next morning, another Sunday, the ship left Brisbane for Sydney. While the men devoured 500 gallons of milk, ice cream and crates of oranges and bananas, Lieutenant Odell walked from deck to deck teaching the patients to sing the famous Australian marching song, "Waltzing Matilda," so we could sing it as we entered Sydney Harbor.

The words to the 1890 song by "Banjo" A.B. Paterson are as follows:

Once a jolly swagman camped by a billabon

Under the shade of a coolibah tree

And he sang as he watched and waited 'til his billy boiled

You'll come a-waltzing matilda with me.

Waltzing matilda, waltzing matilda. You'll come a-waltzing matilda with me. And he sang as he watched and waited 'til his billy boiled. You'll come a-waltzing matilda with me.

Down came a jumbuck to dri-ink at that billabong

Up jumped the swagman and grabbed him with glee

And he sang as he stuffed that jumbuck in his tucker-bag

You'll come a-waltzing matilda with me.

Up rode the squatter, mounted on his thoroughbred

Up rode the troopers, one, two, three

"Where's that jolly jumbruck you've got in your tucker-bag?"

You'll come a-waltzing matilda with me.

Up jumped the swagman and sprang into that billabong

"You'll never take me alive!" said he

And his ghost may be heard as you pa-ass by that billabong

You'll come a-waltzing matilda with me.

In the afternoon, once again on the open seas, the ship's crew and passengers watched the sky cloud to a dark rolling mass on the horizon. The waves rose as thunder rumbled in the distance and lightning crackled through the jet black sky. As the swells grew higher, the ship rode wave after wave in the dark, rising up one steep wave and crashing down into the next.

Many of the patients thought the old ship would break in two as the bow rose out of the sea, followed by the propeller rising with the stern. Everything hung suspended in mid-air for seconds before the cots, chairs and patients crashed again onto the deck.

Once again that evening, Father Shanahan held services on the deck—his last services of the voyage. He finished with a prayer of thanks for keeping the Mactan safe on its journey, then concluded with *The Lord's Prayer*, which everyone joined in praying.

As we sang the closing hymn, we suddenly heard a shout from the port promenade deck:

"Man overboard!"

The bridge rang "full speed a-stern," and started circling back in the rough seas. We used every light we could possibly find, shining it into the dark, churning water for several hours without finding any trace of the missing Filipino soldier, Estanislas Osias, the nineteen-year-old man who had lost one arm and had been unable to communicate with Father Shanahan in either English or Tagalog.

According to Noyer, Ed Mosier, a patient in the next bed, said the Filipino grew more depressed and morose each day, sitting on his cot and staring at the horizon as the storm grew in intensity.

"Then, all of a sudden, he just stood up in his bunk and jumped overboard," Noyer quoted Mosier as saying. "However, he landed in a lifeboat just below the rail. It was unreal. He got up again and jumped out of the life boat and into the sea."

I remember very clearly how rough it was. For two hours, I stood near the front on the right side of the ship, waving spotlights across the mountainous waves as the ship churned around and around in a circle, searching in vain for the man.

Just the yelling of "Man Overboard" is an unbelievable and terrible experience.

The soldier's suicide proved very depressing for Father Shanahan. He was concerned that perhaps his services had brought about the young man's decision to end his problems.

The mood on the ship remained depressed for the next day or two, and the rough seas with heavy winds didn't help matters. It sounded as if the ship were being torn apart.

The violent storm continued to pound the ship the next day as it continued toward Sydney. Waves crashed over the top of the decks, soaking the bedding and the patients.

We kept busy calming the patients, who for the first time showed signs of panic as the pitching ship came out of the water then cracked and popped as it landed with a crash on the next wave. All night long people pulled the cots from the rails and made sure life preservers were at hand.

In his book *Mactan: Ship of Destiny*, Noyer quotes Don Cook as saying: "God must have had His arm around us that night. Yes, He must have had His arm around us because no boat that small could have survived a storm like that without His help."

Sailing into Sydney

THE NEXT MORNING, Tuesday, January 27, sunshine broke through the clouds and the seas slowly calmed as the Mactan headed into Sydney Harbor.

Everyone arose early and I asked that the patients be bathed and shaved. Those who could shave themselves did so; orderlies helped the others. Those who had allowed beards to grow during the month-long journey were told to shave; they were allowed only a small mustache if they so desired.

The men helped each other by sitting in a production line and trimming one another's hair.

We changed each man's dressings and issued a pair of pajamas to each patient. Many of them balked when told they had to wear the brilliant pajamas carefully crafted from sugar bags by the Townsville Red Cross. I had kept them tucked safely under my bunk for just this occasion.

A man would mutter, "I'm not going to wear that."

I would look him in the eye and say, "You're not going to do what? You're putting on those pajamas."

What colors were they? Every color—the color of every flower and every vegetable you can think of. Although some men complained, I insisted till they put them on.

Shortly after noon, we entered the harbor with each patient clean in garishly bright new pajamas and singing loudly from the rear deck the words to "Waltzing Matilda," accompanied by a mouth organ. On the starboard side, according to Noyer, men held themselves erect and with tears streaming down their faces, sang, "God Bless America."

Ships in the harbor saluted the Mactan by ringing bells and tooting whistles. A tug as large as the Mactan pulled the ship to the main deck at Sydney, where a string of ambulances and automobiles awaited. Australian soldiers with cocky hats with brims turned up stood waiting beside stretchers and women in uniform from the Australian Red Cross Motor Corps stood at attention.

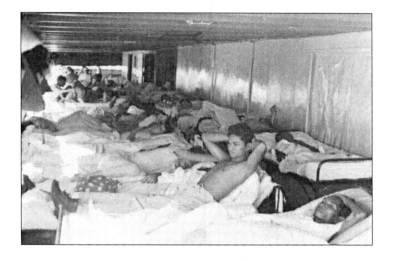

*When the Mactan neared Sydney, I insisted that
each of the patients dress in the bright colored
pajamas given to the ship by the ladies of
Townsville. I also insisted that each man be
shaved.*

The first to board the Mactan was Eliot Palmer, the U.S.
consul general of Australia, and his first assistant, William
Flake, American consul for Sydney. Mr. Palmer invited
the staff to his home for dinner, and to this day we are
friends, keeping in touch at Christmas.

Photographers and reporters also greeted the arrival of the
Mactan, snapping pictures of patients.

Captain Fairfield wrote about arriving in Sydney Harbor,
saying: "They tell us we were given up for lost days ago.
And I thought we were lost last night because it sure was
hell. As it is, we're six hours late in arriving but, by Golly,
we're here and what a relief!"

Within two hours, all of the patients had been removed
from the Mactan and were on their way to the 113th
Australian General Hospital, ten miles outside of town,
where they were given clean beds, good food and a chance
to relax at last on firm ground.

In 1945, author George Korson wrote in *At His Side: The*

Story of the American Red Cross Overseas in World War II:

"Thus ended the long voyage of the first United States hospital ship in World War II. It is impossible in this brief account to detail all the dangers and tensions that lurked around the Mactan every inch and every minute of the way; or to give adequate recognition to the valuable services on board of Father Shanahan, Colonel Carroll and Chief Nurse Ann Fellmeth; or to record fully the devotion and courage of the Filipino doctors and nurses who gave up their homes, families, and livelihoods for the duration to serve on this hospital ship as Red Cross personnel."

Pearl ring from Miriam Fowles

EACH OF THE RED CROSS NURSES had different personalities, but I fared well with each of them. One of the nurses came from Russia, and she kept to herself for the most part. The Filipino nurses tended to spend time together.

Before leaving the ship, Miriam Fowles called me into her room. Miriam, who was in her late forties, was the wife of a British diplomat. She had come to the Philippines from Hong Kong six days before leaving on the Mactan.

She ended up having to rest for about two weeks after the Mactan arrived in Sydney because of the strain and shock of the voyage.

But before she left, she called me into her cabin, where she opened a cloth bag given to her by her mother, an Egyptian who married a British man. She showed me a picture of her mother, who wore beautiful bracelets on the upper part of her arms.

When she opened the bag, I saw gorgeous jewels. She said: "I want to thank you, and I want you to take any piece of jewelry—take anything."

I said, no, I couldn't do that. But she insisted I take a piece, so I took the smallest piece of jewelry—a simple gold ring with two pearls.

"Oh," she said, "no, take something bigger."

Red Cross nurses Miriam Fowles, left, and Katherine Owery are seen on the Mactan. When the journey ended, Miriam asked me to select a piece of her jewelry. I took a small pearl ring, learning much later that the pearls were genuine. Fowles, who came to the Philippines from Hong Kong, lost her husband in the war. She made her home in Australia, where she raised her two grandsons, and died at the age of 93.

I thanked her and said the ring is just fine. "I'll be happy with this."

Later in life, when I worked in Chicago, one of the pearls fell off the ring. So I took it to a jeweler in Chicago and asked if he could replace it.

The jeweler looked at me and said, "Ma'am, you can't afford it."

I said, "What do you mean I can't afford it?"

"That's a genuine pearl! You have lost a genuine pearl. We don't even have them."

He replaced the pearl with a cultured one. When I now look at it, I can't tell which pearl is the original.

Miriam and I kept in touch. She lost her husband during the war. She remarried in Australia and worked at the Sydney Red Cross warehouse supervising supplies to troops in New Guinea until the war ended three years later. She raised her two grandsons.

Her grandson, Daniel, wrote me a letter about his grandmother's death. "She really was incredibly brave," he wrote. "A remarkable lady who had lived a truly remarkable life."

Mactan set a standard

THREE YEARS LATER, while I was in the headquarters, an officer came up to me and said: "Ma'am, weren't you the nurse off the Mactan?"

I can't tell you how many times in my life I've heard that question!

"Yes, I was the nurse on the Mactan."

He said, "I want you to know that I've just attended a conference on hospital ships and they reported that the patients who came off the Mactan were in the best condition of any other ship, including the big ships."

The bright pajamas must have done it.

The first few days in Sydney

AFTER THE PATIENTS HAD LEFT the ship, I decided to stay aboard until the next day when I realized that I had to make arrangements to dispose of all the medication entrusted to me on the voyage. Father Shanahan also offered to stay, so we remained on board the ship for two days and nights. The entire Mactan crew stayed aboard as well.

The day after we docked, Eno Palmer, wife of American Consulate General Eliot E. Palmer at Sydney, came aboard and offered me some of her wearing apparel. She was a woman of very small stature, and during the trip aboard the Mactan, I had lost weight, perhaps ten or fifteen pounds. I weighed only 134, which looked gaunt on my 5-foot-5-inch frame. I'd always been slender but never that thin.

*After the patients left the Mactan, I remained aboard
the ship to keep track of the remaining medicine.
Father Shanahan also stayed, as did the ship's crew.
Mrs. Eno Palmer, wife of Eliot E. Palmer, American
Consulate General at Sydney, came aboard and offered
to loan me some of her clothes. I declined because I
needed to find something to use as a uniform, but
I remained friends with the Palmers, pictured below.*

I thanked her and kindly declined because I needed to go ashore and select an outfit that I could use as a uniform.

The next day an officer from a contingent that had arrived in Australia prior to our landing, perhaps detouring to the continent after the bombing of the Philippines, came aboard the Mactan and offered help. I told him my clothing problem. He had been in Australia long enough to know his way about. I told him I would need to see a financial officer. He said, "No problem." He had a car and took me to the finance officer, where I received my back pay, and then we went shopping.

I found a light-colored shirtwaist dress and added my insignia. That night we dined with a group of his contingent at a popular restaurant.

Topaz jewelry and nightmares

THAT SAME DAY, Father Shanahan and I registered at the city's largest hotel, the same place where Colonel Carroll and Irving Williams were staying. Then we relaxed because our patients were being well taken care of in the Australian hospitals.

The consulate and local dignitaries also hosted Colonel Carroll, Father Shanahan and me.

But at night, asleep in the hotel room bed, I suddenly heard a terrible grinding sound. I thought a big animal had grabbed hold of my arm and I couldn't escape. I awakened with a start, heart pounding and trembling with fear. I realized then where I was and switched on a light before returning to sleep.

I didn't tell anyone about the nightmare, but the following night, I turned on the light before going to sleep. Again I woke up with a start, my heart racing again from the dream of the animal's terrible grinding and its grasp on my arm.

I continued to sleep with the light on for the next several nights and within a week, the nightmare ended.

Later, one of the lieutenants saw me and said: "Ma'am,

After arriving in Sydney, I purchased a set of topaz jewelry that I carried with me tied in a handkerchief throughout Australia and New Guinea, finally bringing the jewelry home to the United States. Below, the Army sent a letter informing my family of my safe arrival in Australia.

IN REPLY REFER TO 𝑆.𝐺.𝑂. SPMCH   jof/en

WAR DEPARTMENT
OFFICE OF THE SURGEON GENERAL
WASHINGTON

May 31, 1942.

Mrs. Henry Fellmeth,
    7029 South Marshfield Avenue,
    Chicago, Illinois.

Dear Mrs. Fellmeth:

        This office has been notified of the safe arrival
in Australia of your daughter, Floramund A. Fellmeth, and our
gratitude for this information is, I believe, second only to
your own.

        We are indeed proud of the heroism and devotion to
duty which the nurses in the Philippines have displayed and our
hopes and prayers are for their safety and well-being.

                        Sincerely yours,

                        Julia O. Flikke,
                        Colonel, A.U.S.,
                        Superintendent, A.N.C.

you look so much better."

His comment surprised me.

"You knew exactly what you meant, but when I looked at you, it was as if your eyes were hollow," he said. "The expression in your eyes was far away."

I had been ordering supplies and preparing uniforms, taking care of business. Other than a few nightmares, I'd weathered the adventure aboard the Mactan rather well.

One time, walking past a shop in Sydney, I saw a set of beautiful topaz jewelry in the window. The first time I saw that jewel was on the ring of a surgeon at St. Elizabeth's Hospital in Chicago. When I had asked him what it was, he told me "smoky topaz."

In Australia certain items could be sold only a few hours a day, which were the same hours I was on duty. But coming off duty one night, I saw a man in the store and knocked on the window. Because I was an American in uniform, he opened the door and invited me in. We negotiated for a necklace, bracelet and ring, all adorned with topaz stones from China. I bought the set and carried the jewelry with me tied in a handkerchief until I returned home.

Father writes to the Fellmeths

ON THE DAY I FLEW TO MELBOURNE, February 5, Father Shanahan wrote a letter to my parents in Chicago, describing our trip aboard the Mactan and me in particular. Here's what it said:

February 5, 1942

C/o American Consulate General

7 Wyngard Street

Sydney, Australia

Dear Mr. and Mrs. Fellmeth:

There is no need for me or anyone else to

After the Mactan arrived safely, Father Shanahan wrote a beautiful letter to the Fellmeths in Chicago singing the praises of their daughter, Floramund.

step up and tell you that you have a grand girl in your daughter, Floramund. I must do it anyway, for I see this as one of the few ways whereby I can somehow repay her for her invaluable assistance to me on the Red Cross Hospital Ship from the Philippines down to Australia.

I am a Catholic priest, an American Jesuit, who stepped from College work in Manila into this war as Chaplain with the American Red Cross. To step aboard a Hospital Ship with but three hours notice was a change that I could not easily cope with, were it not for your daughter, who from the very first moment of meeting did so much to put Father at his ease.

It was soon easy to see that the young lady knew her way around in her work, in spite of the unusual conditions in which we all found ourselves. As the Chaplain in his work depends a great deal upon the nurse, I was fortunate to meet with one who knew the right answers, and gave them off in a very forthright manner.

The little lady was ever ready to help, so much so, that I might have forgotten at times that she is a woman and found myself at any time readily calling upon her for assistance or advice in getting around one or another problem that would come up. Were it necessary, I could get Colonel Carroll, the doctor, and Mr. Irving Williams of the American Red Cross to give the same testimony. We admired her ability and did not hesitate to call upon this directly generous skill of hers.

I, myself, experienced the kindness of her nursing skill, for my elbow picked up an infection on the trip. Were I one of her own family, she could not have been more solicitous. This unending devotion to her patients robbed her of much needed sleep many and many a night.

How she kept going, and still maintained her glorious sense of humor, was a mystery and a joy to us all.

The four of us Americans of the staff ate together. Here was the time for relaxation from hospital work. Let it be said that your daughter was the center of most of the humor attempted by us, the three men. We teased her considerably. We liked it, though I doubt, if she always did. How she could stand it at all, I don't know, for we found ourselves always ganging up on her. It was our heavy handed way of letting her know that she was the center of our gathering. Did she see it this way? I don't know. At any rate the three of us respected her thoroughly, while liking her very much.

Once she told me, while putting an application on my infected elbow, that when she gets home, she will have at least one good talk with her father and mother, for she has something she will want to tell them. I said to her then and there that I could tell her what she would say to them. She put that caustic eye of her's upon me. So I had to get to work, but it was easy. ...

I assure you that she is well, rested, and enjoying herself considerably. Apparently she is on her way to important work. Have no fear she is eminently capable—and with very good friends. For all this she can thank her mother and father, her brothers and her sisters, who gave her such an excellent start.

I might well bring this to an apt ending with a "Thank you" for her.

Sincerely,

(Signed) Thomas A. Shanahan, S.J.

Hailed as a hero

AFTER ARRIVING IN AUSTRALIA and notifying my family of my safety, I soon discovered that the Mactan's journey made headlines in America and Australia. In April, when General MacArthur cited me for bravery and presented me to the press corps in Melbourne, Australia, I found myself surrounded by reporters asking questions— about the Philippines, the Mactan's journey, the Japanese, the war.

I always tried to acknowledge and comment on the bravery and resourcefulness of the American nurses who helped the wounded. The *Chicago Herald American* newspaper quotes me as saying:

"We did an around-the-clock job in Bataan, but why shouldn't we? The boys fighting didn't get any time off. We got up early, worked through the day and then, just when we thought we might get a chance to sleep, a Jap raid would begin and we would work through the night.

"Lots of times we went for days without even getting a chance to take off our clothes. And most of the girls, remember, got into service and into action so rapidly that their nurses' uniforms have not yet caught up with them. It's much harder to do your work in civilian dress."

The *Chicago Sun* printed this quotation from me:

"There wasn't a nurse of Bataan who was flinching. If they were on duty at the time of a raid they stayed on duty. We often went without sleep for days. For a little time, when the heavy raids first started, the girls got a bit down, but after the bombing had been going on, they got used to it and their spirits went up wonderfully."

The *Chicago Herald American*, on April 11, 1942, blasted across the top of the front page in bold red lettering: "Hail Chicago War Heroine"

The article went on to state: "MacArthur Hails Chicago Heroine" and featured a picture of me on the front page, with the caption below that read: "Praised for bravery."

My father used to take that newspaper and fold it with the

Hail Chicago War Heroine

Herald ☆ American — CHICAGO

RACING
OPENING MARKETS

MacArthur
Hails Chicago
Heroine

After the Mactan arrived safely in Australia, newspaper headlines hailed me as a hero in my Chicago hometown. I also was listed as No. 20 in an article about twenty-six "Catholics who made the news in 1942."

HEROINE'S PARENTS

MacArthur Hails Chicago Hero Nurse

*My father, left, and
mother, below,
proudly marched in a
Chicago parade in
March carrying
United States flags.
My father often
walked to the
neighboring stores
with the newspaper
tucked under his arm,
with the red banner
headline hailing
his daughter as a hero
quite visible
for all to see.*

**MacArthur Cites
Her for Bravery**

red headlines facing out whenever he went shopping. He'd walk up Ashland Street and shop, always carrying that newspaper. Even during times of rationing, my father received everything he asked for. Daddy never needed coupons or ration cards, and bless them if they didn't ask about his daughter!

Another headline, in the April 12, 1942, edition of the *Chicago Sun*, stated: "'Baby' of Chicago Family Is Lieutenant in Army." The article describes my promotion in March to First Lieutenant Floramund Fellmeth. The article described me as the senior nurse attached to General Douglas MacArthur's headquarters in Australia.

I was also listed as No. 20 in a list of twenty-six "Catholics who made the news in 1942" in the company of Pope Pius XII; President Manuel Quezon of the Philippines; George M. Cohan, actor and playwright; and Carlton Hayes, U.S. ambassador to Spain. My listing read: "Army Nurse Floramund Fellmeth, cited for bravery at Bataan."

A bit of survivor's guilt

I FELT RELIEVED TO FIND SAFETY in Australia, but later on I also felt a little guilty about the nurses left behind in the Philippines—many of whom became prisoners of the Japanese. Some of the nurses left Corregidor in late April on a submarine, but sixty-six Army nurses became prisoners, as well as eleven Navy nurses. Many of those incarcerated had been my close friends.

Army nurses evacuated from Corregidor in 1942 included Catherine M. Acorn, Dorothea M. Daley, Leona Gastinger, Susan Downing, Nancy J. Gillahan, Grace D. Hallman, Eunice C. Hatchitt, Willa Hook, Ressa Jenkins, Harriet G. Lee, Mary G. Lohr, Florence MacDonald, Hortense McKay, Mary L. Moultrie, Mollie A. Peterson, Juanita Redmond, Mabel V. Stevens, Ruth W. Straub, Helen Summers, Beth A. Veley and Lucy Wilson. Navy nurse Ann Bernatitus also was evacuated from the Philippines.

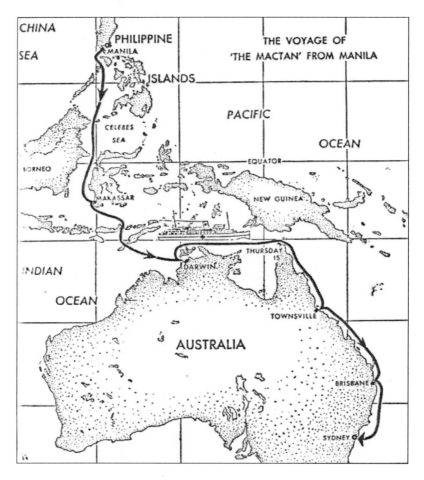

CHINA
SEA

PHILIPPINE
MANILA

ISLANDS

THE VOYAGE OF
'THE MACTAN' FROM MANILA

CELEBES
SEA

PACIFIC

OCEAN

BORNEO

EQUATOR

MAKASSAR

NEW GUINEA

INDIAN

OCEAN

THURSDAY
IS

DARWIN

TOWNSVILLE

AUSTRALIA

BRISBANE

SYDNEY

The map above, from George Korson's book At
His Side: The American Red Cross
Overseas in World War II, *shows the route
the Mactan took to reach Australia.*

Patients after the Mactan

WHEN THE SHIP FINALLY DOCKED safely in Sydney,
Noyer wrote that 210 of the original 224 patients
gave a petition to Red Cross director Irving Williams simply stating their thanks for the safe passage, from "the
orphans of the Philippines Fiasco." Along the twenty-
seven-day voyage over 4,965 miles, three patients lost
their lives—one in surgery, another from critical wounds

and a third by suicide. When they arrived in Sydney, eleven other patients were too ill to write their names on the petition, Noyer said. Four of those men later died in Sydney.

In the document, the patients stated: "We, the undersigned officers and enlisted men of the USAFFE, in grateful appreciation of the services rendered by the Philippine Chapter of the American Red Cross under the supervision of Mr. Irving Williams, Field Director, wish by this letter to express our gratitude. The evacuation of the wounded soldiers from Manila by the Red Cross prior to its occupation by the enemy was instrumental in preserving the lives and health of the undersigned."

The patients signing the document listed their ranks and home addresses.

They had reason to be grateful. Upon arriving at Sydney, the Mactan was declared unseaworthy. (Later, the U.S. Army converted her to serve as a floating barracks for small ships' crews in New Guinea.)

A year after the journey aboard the Mactan, I received a package in the mail from Father Shanahan. I opened the package to discover my extra uniform, cleaned and neatly pressed, with a note that stated: "They have seen their duty and need to be returned to their rightful owner."

I gave the uniform to my father, who wore the outfit all the time to go shopping or do the cooking. He'd wear the khaki pants and walk up Ashland with the newspaper tucked under one arm.

Irving Williams and MacArthur

IRVING WILLIAMS DISCUSSED the Mactan's voyage with General MacArthur in March 1942. Wondering aloud, he asked the general why the Japanese didn't attack the hospital ship, and the general reportedly described the Mactan as "a test case—the first dealing of the Japanese with a hospital ship," according to Noyer.

Williams said the general also didn't seem surprised when

The photo above shows members of the Philippine Red Cross who sailed aboard the Mactan to care for patients. Included are nurses Maria Perez, Dolores Bolante, Visitacion Cortes, Katherine Owery, Miriam Fowles, Mercedes Santos, Elisa Domingo, Salud F. Valencerina, Maxima Corpus and Basilia Hernando; Doctors Bernardo Limlingan, Federico Roman, Conrado Topacio, Manuel Escudero Jr., Gregorio P. Chua and Irineo Pantangco; male nurses Apolinar Sanchez and Pedro Carpio; and attendants George N. Goloobeff and Benjamin N. Setias.

told the Mactan had been declared unseaworthy. According to Noyer, Williams quoted the general as saying: "I knew that before you left. Valdes told me so—said it was suicide. But she was the only available ship and we had to get those men out. It was an epochal trip... God and the element of surprise protected you."

Williams continued working as Red Cross field director in Australia and New Guinea until the end of the war, and in July 1946, he was awarded the Medal of Freedom "for meritorious and humanitarian service to the United States in the Southwest Pacific area... Upon being selected to assist in the evacuation of the wounded from the Philippines, he served with conspicuous merit aboard a hospital ship on a most hazardous voyage from the Philippines to Australia..."

Father Shanahan's promotion

B Y THE TIME THE JOURNEY aboard the Mactan ended, Colonel Carroll and I had convinced Father Shanahan to become an Army chaplain. He consulted with his superior, the Jesuit vice provincial in Melbourne, who agreed to the idea, then applied to join the Army.

A newspaper article describing Father Shanahan's commission in the Army stated that when the paperwork arrived on General MacArthur's desk to give Father Shanahan the rank of first lieutenant in the Army, the general read the name and asked: "Isn't this the Father Shanahan who was chaplain of the Mactan?"

When an aide assured him that it was the same man, the general crossed out the words "first lieutenant" and said: "Make Father Shanahan a captain!" Then he signed the altered form.

Father Shanahan served in northern Australia, then as deputy chaplain in charge of supplies for Melbourne, Sydney and Brisbane. He accompanied General MacArthur on his return to Leyte, and on February 5, 1945, he was with the conquering American troops when

Jesuit from the Philippines now in Melbourne

Rev. T. Shanahan, S.J.

A RECENT interesting arrival in Melbourne is the Rev. Thomas Shanahan, S.J., a native of Waterbury, Connecticut, U.S.A., whose fate caused grave concern to his relatives and fellow-Jesuits in the United States during the Japanese invasion of the Philippines. Fr. Shanahan was reported wounded, but subsequently turned up in Australia, and last week visited the office of "The Advocate."

Fr. Shanahan arrived in Australia as chaplain on a Red Cross ship carrying wounded soldiers.

Fr. Shanahan was assigned to the Red Cross Emergency Hospital in the Customs House of the Manila Port Area. On Christmas Eve at noon he was in the Port Area, which was an object of Japanese bombing.

On New Year's Eve, when the American Red Cross was running out a ship with wounded American and Filipino soldiers, Fr. Shanahan was the chaplain. Three other Americans made up the staff, the doctor in charge, the head nurse, the head of the American Red Cross in the Military and Naval Field Work. The rest of the staff were Filipino doctors and nurses.

Fr. Shanahan taught Philosophy and the Classics at his alma mater, Holy Cross College, Worcester, Mass., U.S.A., for some six years before returning to the Philippines in 1940. He had spent three years in the Philippines as a scholastic before his ordination. During most of his time in the Philippines he taught at the Ateneo de Manila, the Jesuit University in Manila, which at the outbreak of the war numbered 2000 students. The Ateneo has long been called the "West Point of the Philippines." Its military system became famous throughout the islands. It is estimated that 1000 of its graduates were officers with the Filipino forces defending their country.

Father Shanahan's role aboard the Mactan also made news.

they returned to Manila. He was the first chaplain to enter the Santo Tomas concentration camp and earned a Bronze star for organizing relief and ministering to battle casualties in frontline hospitals.

He wrote me another letter in 1946, and in it he referred to the relationship among Irving Williams (Red Cross), Colonel Percy Carroll, Father Shanahan and me. In it, he said: "Was it not a blessing that the four of us on the Mactan staff got along so beautifully and that it all looks better as the years roll along. I can be a nasty fault finder. But in this case, everything was perfect. Thank God."

Father Shanahan died in Boston in 1963 at age sixty-eight.

PRIEST, MANILA HERO, PROMOTED CAPTAIN BY GEN. MacARTHUR

NEW YORK, Dec. 1.—The story of a signal honor bestowed by General MacArthur upon Father Thomas Shanahan, S.J., has been communicated to the Most Rev. John F. O'Hara, C. S. C., Military Delegate, by a chaplain just arrived from Australia.

Father Shanahan, originally reported wounded in the bombing of Manila, actually went as Chaplain of the ship "Mactan" bearing the wounded from the Philippines to Australia.

On the eve of the fall of Manila, General MacArthur was anxious to evacuate all the wounded. Despite great difficulties this was accomplished. The Inter-island Steamship "Mactan" was converted into a Red Cross ship. A number of doctors and nurses were assembled and the wounded were transferred late on the eve of New Year's Day. At the last moment it was discovered that no chaplain had been appointed.

This part of the story has been supplied by the four Filipino nurses who are at present in New York, having come all the way with the wounded men from Australia. They were among the nurses sent to the "Mactan" to take care of the wounded in the course of the voyage to Australia. They told how Father Shanahan came to be appointed chaplain of the "Mactan." According to the nurses, he had been very active during the bombing of Manila, especially in the port area where the bombing was most intense, and his name was well known to the military personnel, especially of the Medical Corps. When he was asked to accompany the "Mactan"

same man, General MacArthur crossed out the words "First Lieutenant" on the commission and said, "Make Father Shanahan a Captain!"

as chaplain, he had about five minutes' preparation, just long enough to call Father Hurley, his Superior, and obtain his permission to leave.

When the trip was over and the wounded had been taken care of in Australia, Father Shanahan consulted the Jesuit Vice-Provincial in Melbourne with regard to his future duties. It was agreed that Father Shanahan should make application to become a regular army chaplain.

When General MacArthur arrived in Australia he found a great deal of desk work awaiting him. Some new commissions had been held up pending his approval. In going through these he found the regular form, made out but awaiting his signature, commissioning Father Shanahan as First Lieutenant in the Army of the United States. General MacArthur read the name and then inquired, "Isn't this the Father Shanahan who was chaplain of the 'Mactan'?" On being assured that he was the

This newspaper article described the circumstances of Father Shanahan's promotion.

During the one-year anniversary of the Mactan's voyage, passengers and crew gathered again.
In the top photo, from left, are William Slicer, Father Shanahan, me, Colonel Carroll, Miriam Fowles and Doctor Howard Angell (both of the Red Cross), Air Corps Captain Frederic Stanton (the photographer) and Irving Williams, Red Cross director.
At left, I am holding a flower replica of the Mactan.

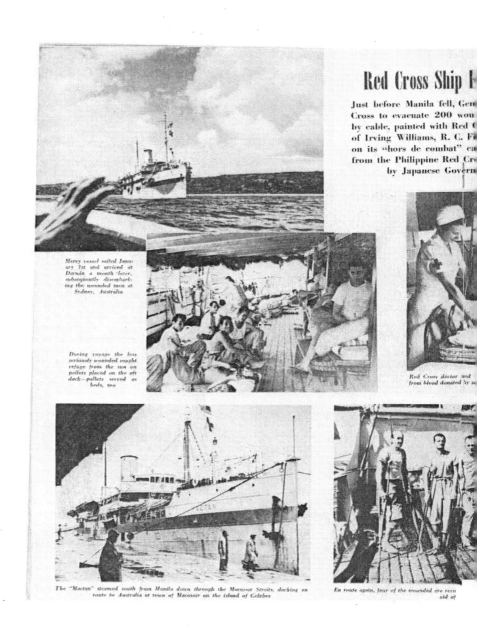

The May 1942 issue of the Red Cross Courier printed
photos of the Mactan's journey as it centerpiece.

acuates Manila Wounded

al MacArthur asked the American Red
led men. The *Mactan* was chartered
oss flags and emblem. Under direction
d Director at Manila, the *Mactan* took
go, was staffed with doctors and nurses
s Chapter. Safe conduct was accorded
ent despite rumors to contrary

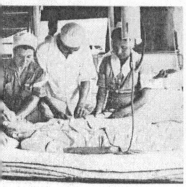

ses give emergency transfusion aboard ship, using plasma made
American who contributed to the Red Cross donor bank to supply
military and civilian needs

American flag was still flying over Manila when this Red Cross
banner was raised below Stars and Stripes on the "Mactan"

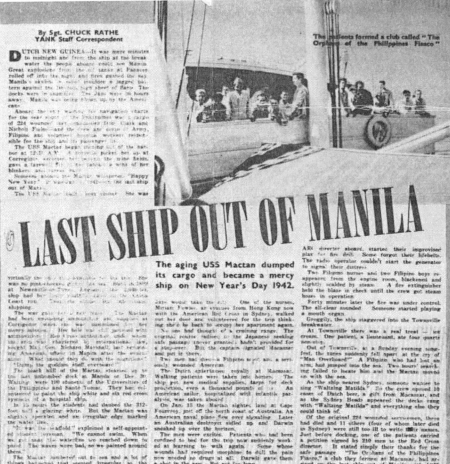

By Sgt. CHUCK RATHE
YANK Staff Correspondent

The patients formed a club called "The Orphans of the Philippines Fiasco"

LAST SHIP OUT OF MANILA

The aging USS Mactan dumped its cargo and became a mercy ship on New Year's Day 1942.

Near the war's end, after Allied troops returned to the Philippines, YANK staff correspondent Sgt. Chuck Rathe wrote a piece for The Army-Navy News *about the journey of the Mactan in January 1942.*

Chapter Seven

Americans in Australia

Establishing US Army Medical Services

As the first Army nurse in Sydney, I helped Colonel Percy J. Carroll establish the Army Medical Corps in Australia. I am seen in Brisbane feeding kangaroos and at left with a koala bear.

Assignment in Australia

O N FEBRUARY 5, 1942, I took my first airplane flight to
Melbourne, Australia, with Colonel Carroll to establish our headquarters in an empty school within walking
distance of the Victoria Barracks, the Australian headquarters. One day, I joined the Australian Army and Air Group
Nurses in being among the first women to dine at the barracks.

The United States needed to establish Army medical
services in Melbourne. I helped set up the first surgeons'
office and a small clinic, then waited for the first group of
nurses to arrive in Australia from the United States. We
received temporary duty—Colonel Carroll as a surgeon
and me as acting chief nurse. We established U.S. Medical
Headquarters in Melbourne. Colonel Carroll assumed a
desk job, and on February 7 I found myself—at 26½ years
of age—the first chief nurse of the U.S. Army Forces in
Australia.

Five days after arriving in Melbourne, we learned that 232
nurses were at sea, sailing from New York for Melbourne.
We prepared for their arrival, finding transportation and
housing at three convalescent homes and a 116-room
hotel. We worked with the Australian army to prepare the
lodging.

By February 20, 1942, we'd started a dispensary at the
port of debarkation. After more nurses arrived, two were
assigned temporary duty at the dispensary.

While the American medical department was being established, all U.S. patients received treatment at Australian
military hospitals.

The United States medical department was not prepared
for the nurses who arrived in civilian clothes—eventually
nearly 2,000 women. It fell to me to design uniforms and
have them made. I ordered uniforms and the manufactur-
ing of brass buttons.

As supply officer for all women's uniforms and needs, I
eventually supplied even the Women's Army Corps. But
as I went about my duties, I often thought about my col-

leagues left behind at Bataan and Corregidor, and worried about how they were faring in the war zone.

Other nurses arrive

ON FEBRUARY 19, we learned of the Japanese air raid on Darwin, during which the enemy fired on several U.S. Army hospitals and an Australian hospital ship. The Army troops moved south and evacuated Darwin.

February 26, 1942, proved to be a glorious day when 233 members of the United States Army Nurse Corps arrived on Australian shores. They would be working in U.S. Army hospitals that were being established throughout the country.

The nurses, who had boarded the ship in civilian dress, were told to bring with them only one change of clothing. They were told their uniforms would be supplied at a port of debarkation. So when I met the nurses, they were full of questions about uniforms, pay allowances, allotments and other details.

The 9th Station Hospital received thirty-one of the nurses, but no assigned chief nurse. However, chief nurse Francis McClelland, a first lieutenant in the ANC, oversaw nursing at the 52nd Evacuation Hospital, where fifty-two of the nurses were assigned. First Lieutenant Olga Benderoff served as chief nurse at the 4th General Hospital, where 120 of the nurses would work, and Elizabeth Deschenes, a second lieutenant, supervised thirty nurses assigned to the 109th Station Hospital.

A finance warrant officer helped me by making out pay vouchers and within three days each nurse had been interviewed and paid.

They received a week to recuperate after their strenuous six-week voyage, then in March nearly half of the new nurses—those assigned to the 52nd, 9th and 4th hospitals—sailed from Melbourne with the Poppy Force, the division-sized task force that secured New Caledonia and other areas. I was still the only nurse assigned to the U.S. headquarters.

The Australian nursing services continued doing all in their power to make the nurses' stay a comfortable and happy one.

Promoted to chief nurse

ON TUESDAY, MARCH 10, 1942, COLONEL Carroll called me into his office, where he had gathered with the senior staff. He informed me of my temporary promotion to first lieutenant, which automatically made me a chief nurse. I felt shocked by the promotion.

The colonel proceeded to remove my very special gold second lieutenant's bars and pinned on shiny new silver ones. The group in the office, with smiles on their faces, came forward to shake my hand.

But I turned my attention to the colonel.

"You can't do this to me!" I shouted, pounding my fist on his desk. "You have isolated me! I'm going to be a chief nurse and no one will have anything to do with me."

He simply smiled and responded: "Well, I have done it."

As a chief nurse, I no longer shared lodgings or social activities with nurses because I had to supervise them.

Our 201 records, or duty records, covered the system of grading, starting at one and increasing by fractions until it reached the number seven, where education and performance were taken into consideration. A registered nurse started at three points and our first grading began six months after joining the service. Salary increased from $70 a month initially as a second lieutenant to $90 a month after a few years. Your salary increased with promotions and time of service. (Our salaries were not equal to those of male officers but that changed after World War II).

Chief nurses became first lieutenants. At that time, the Army Nurse Corps had only one major, Julia O. Flikke, superintendent of the ANC in Washington, D.C.; five captains at general hospitals and then first lieutenants. Later the ANC offered more ranks for promotions, including generals.

Finding an adequate outfit to serve as a uniform proved to be one of my first orders of business upon arriving in Sydney. I designed this uniform with a detachable, washable collar for myself and the nurses who would soon follow. The uniforms took only a month to complete.

So on March 10, 1942, I was appointed acting chief nurse of Headquarters United States Army Forces in the South Pacific. I took the oath of office as a first lieutenant in the United States Army March 14, 1942. There was no going back. Giving up the gold bars changed my life.

It had never entered my mind to become a chief nurse, although others told me later they always knew I would be one. But I neither desired nor sought the promotion; it just happened. I did know I was an outstanding surgical nurse.

My social life didn't completely wither away. I continued seeing movies and attending theater presentations and social functions with a group of people.

Spring 1942

THE U.S. ARMY SURGEON'S OFFICE took over the new Royal Melbourne hospital, which was nearing completion. The 4th General Hospital planned to use a completed nursing home as a hospital, and the nurses' living quarters occupied the top two floors.

We also learned 344 additional nurses were heading to Australia. I assigned two additional nurses—Second Lieutenants Sophia Haas and Olive King—to the dispensary at the port of debarkation. The Poppy Force, a division-sized task force, asked headquarters to promote Mary Johnson to chief nurse at the 9th Station Hospital, since the unit had left without a chief nurse.

As for the uniforms, we had only one blue field uniform, a few capes and coats. The Poppy Force took Air Corps type coveralls for each nurse because that proved more practical on the front line.

Among the hospital supplies received in March were about a hundred pairs of "duty" shoes, which would help a great deal.

I worked with the quartermaster in locating a material manufacturer, a clothes manufacturer and a wholesale jeweler to obtain the buttons for our uniforms. After conferring with Lieutenant Olga Benderoff, we decided to hold an Easter Day Review wearing our new uniforms. She organized Parade practice, which helped fill time as the nurses spent every spare moment of the day concentrating on marching and saluting. But a delay in obtaining the buttons pushed our scheduled review a week past Easter.

We'd hear about the needs of our nurses in the Philippines, growing greater as the days passed. On March 25, I met with Miss Dunn, an American representing American women in Australia, and Mrs. McDougall, an Australian from the War Nurses Comforts Fund, to see what we could do to help.

On March 30, eighty of our nurses attended tea at Government House, hosted by the very charming and natural Lady Duggan, president of the Victorian branch of the Australian Red Cross. We learned that the women working for the Red Cross received no wages.

The next day, March 31, Mr. Gamble of the American Red Cross came to discuss the supplies needed by our nurses in the Philippines, which the Red Cross agreed to buy. An Australian working through the quartermaster did the purchasing.

Meanwhile, Colonel Carroll—as surgeon of the U.S. Army Forces in Australia (USAFIA), the highest U.S. Army command in the Southwest Pacific area—spent the month determining how many medical personnel he needed and making requests for additional staff, according to a 1963 report on the "Medical Department, United States Army in World War II, Organization and Administration in World War II," written by Blanche B. Armfield, M.A., and prepared under the direction of Lieutenant General Leonard D. Heaton, surgeon general, United States Army. Colonel Carroll asked for hospitals, airplane ambulances, dental laboratories as well as medical and dental supplies. He needed anesthetics, blood plasma, quinine and other medical supplies for the forces in the Philippines.

The Australians provided many medical supplies and hospitalized U.S. Army patients—as many as 16,500 in May and June of 1942.

On April 1, I spoke with Colonel Galloway and an Australian debarkation officer about moving some of our nurses. Those in the 4th General Hospital needed to move to the Royal Melbourne Hospital April 4, and Lady Duggan and her colleagues promised to have convalescent homes made ready for the incoming nurses.

The next day, a call came from Camp Darley, about forty miles away, for two nurses. With the increase in our soldiers there, the number of patients overwhelmed the three Australian nurses in charge of the camp hospital. So we assigned ten nurses to temporary duty at Camp Darley, including Second Lieutenant Mary K. Murphy as the chief nurse. They left on the afternoon train to relieve the three Australian nurses.

Meanwhile, back in the Philippines, Captain Maude C.

This plaque is all that remains of Camp Darley, about forty miles from Melbourne, where many Dutch and American forces were stationed during the war. Wally and I visited the site in the 1980s.

Davison wrote in my 201 records on April 3, 1942, from Station Hospital, Fort Mills, Philippine Islands, that: "Up to date no word has been received at this station as to Miss Fellmeth's whereabouts." Lieutenant Florence MacDonald brought my 201 records with her in late April 1942 when she escaped from the Philippines to Darwin, Australia, aboard a PBY.

On Easter Sunday, April 5, 1942, in Melbourne, we spent a quiet day. After Mass most of the nurses went to the American hospitality center for breakfast. I received a letter from my sister Claire and her friend Hazel, featuring calla lilies as symbols of Easter and the resurrection.

"Your return from the perils of war is equally symbolic of the resurrection, brought right down to where we can all understand and appreciate the true meaning of Easter," Hazel wrote.

"These lilies, from Claire and myself, are an expression of our understanding of your great courage, faith and love of

After finally receiving our full uniforms, we held a review of the U.S. Army nurses where the press snapped photos. In the top photo, I am standing with the male officers watching the review. At center, I am second from the left. And below, a Herald Feature Service photographer also took our picture when we attended Mass. I am seen at left.

humanity which sustained you thru your hours of trial and brought you back as a living symbol of the greatness of the human spirit which cannot be conquered by brute force nor destroyed by instruments of war."

They sent their love and prayers for safety as I carry out my appointed mission in life.

On Tuesday, April 7, thirty nurses arrived at Brisbane—the 5th Station Hospital—with a chief nurse, Miss Bateman, and another thirty went to the 53rd Station Hospital with chief nurse Miss Chase. Eight nurses were assigned to the 1st Evacuation Hospital and ten to the 33rd Surgery Hospital, for a total of seventy-eight nurses.

Two days later, I spent most of the day at the docks waiting for the convoy from the States, but discovered at 11 P.M. that the ship wouldn't dock until the next morning.

So Friday morning at 6:30 A.M., Major Rose and I were at the pier to greet the nurses, who debarked after 9 A.M. We had fifty nurses assigned to the 33rd Surgery Hospital under Miss Brandon as chief nurse; sixty assigned to the 28th Surgery Hospital under Miss Kirby; forty-four assigned under Miss Watkins to the 1st Evacuation Hospital; fifty-two assigned to the 10th Evacuation Hospital under the supervision of Miss Gunn; thirty sent to the 47th Station Hospital with Miss Parker and twenty-nine assigned to the 12th Station Hospital under Miss Egner. Altogether, 265 nurses left the ship to help the American Army hospitals in Australia.

By Saturday, April 11, eighty-one of the uniform coats arrived and the nurses from the 4th General Hospital stayed up late fitting uniforms. It took only a month to complete the uniforms, which included casting and making the buttons and insignias—the first made for the Army in the Southwest Pacific.

The next morning, Sunday, April 12, the nurses attended church in a group, and for many it was the first time they appeared in uniform. The 4th General Hospital nurses had their first review and it was a grand sight! The Australian press captured the moment in photos. It was a proud and thrilling day for all of us.

Captain Clement arrives

THE FOLLOWING DAY, APRIL 13, I was on my way out to greet the arriving ships when I met two women on the stairs of the Army headquarters building. Captain Martha Jane Clement of the Army Nurse Corps introduced herself and First Lieutenant Mildred Dunmore.

I answered: "Now I can go home." However, after she and Colonel Carroll met, they decided I should remain in Australia, in charge of all women's supplies.

That meant the staff at the Army headquarters included me, a first lieutenant and ANC assistant director; Mrs. M. J. Clement, captain ANC, director; and Miss A.M. Dunmore, a first lieutenant and ANC assistant director.

By this time, the number of nurses in Australia totaled 466, including three at the headquarters in Melbourne, 120 at the 4th General Hospital, forty-eight in Brisbane and 295 in Melbourne.

Thirty nurses who had originally landed at Brisbane from the States arrived at Melbourne for training, then left again in a few days for Perth.

My social life featured visits with political figures, including Mrs. Dickaner, an American consul's wife, where we talked about the hospitality center. The headquarters nursing staff, accompanied by Miss Benderoff, also went to a tea at the Scotts Hotel given by the War Nurses Comforts Fund in honor of Australian nurses who returned from the Far East. I also remained friends with Eno and Eliot Palmer, the American Consulate General at Sydney.

I accompanied Captain Clement and Miss Dunmore to visit all the nurses in Melbourne, so they could meet their new director.

At noon on Friday, April 17, the 1st Evacuation Hospital nurses going to Brisbane and the 12th Station Hospital and 33rd Surgical Hospital nurses going to Townsville sailed on the Santa Paula. In the late afternoon, the 5th Station Hospital nurses left by train for Sydney, where they planned to take a boat to Perth.

On Saturday, I accompanied First Lieutenants Dunmore and Benderoff (chief nurse of the 4th General Hospital) to Camp Darley for an inspection of the hospital and nurses' homes there, thirty-eight miles from Melbourne. We found conditions favorable.

On April 19, I met with Colonel Carroll and his headquarters staff to discuss the organization. The next day, we inspected the nurses' quarters and visited sick nurses at the 4th General Hospital, which was still in a state of construction, rendering a handicap for the living conditions of the nurses. We found the sick nurses were improving.

During April, the Allies lost the Netherlands East Indies to the Japanese.

But on April 18, General MacArthur assumed command of all forces of the United States, United Kingdom, Australia and the Netherlands in the Southwest Pacific. President Roosevelt had ordered MacArthur to Australia so the Japanese in the Philippines wouldn't capture him. When he left in March 1942, the general promised Filipinos: "I shall return." He kept his promise by returning in the fall of 1944.

Press conference for the nurses

AT 11 A.M. APRIL 20, we held a press conference with Australian and American correspondents, who asked the nurses questions about their arrival and life in Australia. I wound up as the chief spokesperson for the group of nurses.

A resulting article on April 20, 1942, in *WOMAN*, featured the headline: "U.S. Nurses Here Forswear Marriage For Duty," and went on to describe the requirements and regulations governing military nurses.

It stated that many of the nurses left for Australia with only twenty-four hours' notice under sealed orders with small suitcases. They must be graduated nurses, over twenty-one, single with a high school education and American citizenship. They enter as second lieutenants,

By ELIZABETH HANSON

Mutual Broadcasting System's Frank "Babs" Cuhel, top left, seated with a Navy officer, interviewed me in the middle of the night after I arrived on the Mactan. He died in a 1943 plane crash. A newspaper article in April 1942 features U.S. Army nurses.

with other ranks listed at first lieutenant, captain and major.

The article stated the nurses may not marry during wartime and can date only commissioned officers, but they can wear makeup and nail polish, even on duty. American nurses can smoke and drink, with discretion. And the first consideration of the nurses upon arrival was purchasing silk stockings, since silk and nylon—the silk substitute—had been rationed in the United States.

While the Army Nurse Corps in peacetime consisted of about a thousand nurses, during World War II the number swelled to 10,000.

The reporter quoted me describing conditions on the battlefields of Bataan and Corregidor, where many of my colleagues still struggled to survive.

"There we often worked sixteen hours at a stretch and spent days together when there was neither time nor opportunity to take off our clothes. Just as one managed to get a few hours off duty it seemed to be time for another raid."

I also spoke about the bravery of the nurses under fire.

"The girls did, and are still doing, a marvelous job. They didn't flinch from the most appalling tasks and ordeals. At least one base hospital was bombed twice by the Japs, but the staff continued to work calmly, as though nothing unusual were happening."

I also told about a nurse who still made a point of rising earlier than everyone else so she could set the nurses' and patients' food trays artistically and attractively to show no traces of havoc. "I think we all tried to create, as much as was possible, a peacetime atmosphere."

The article also described the uniforms that I'd been charged with creating. Despite some delay waiting for the uniforms to be fitted with regulation brass buttons, the nurses all now wore black oxford shoes, natural-colored silk stockings and the same outfit—"smart navy blue reefer top coat, navy tunic jacket, lighter blue skirt, and snappy forage cap trimmed with maroon pipings." In the field, they wore a light blue dress and white cap.

After the press conference, I went to the Victoria Barracks to meet the surgeon general of the Australian Army, then returned to headquarters for a 4:30 P.M. medical staff conference with Colonel Carroll and Captain Clement.

A letter from Australia

ON APRIL 25, 1942, *The Army and Navy Journal* published a letter I had written to the superintendent of the Army Nurse Corps, Colonel Julia O. Flikke, describing conditions in the Philippines and at the United States Army Forces Headquarters in Australia as well as the arrival of the American nurses.

Dear Mrs. Flikke,

December the eighth—that infamous day; it would seem that an eternity would be needed for all the events that occurred. The Philippines and our nurses there, shall remain vividly in my mind for the rest of my life. You can be so very proud of the girls I had to leave behind; their job is immense and they are doing it magnificently.

After the first bombs fell there was so much work to do. We were annoyed because of the precious time we lost when we had to abandon the hospital and go to the trenches. The question of uniforms arose; white was too good a target and besides our uniforms were dirty after the first trip to the ground. Our blues would have been more serviceable, but our enemy was also wearing that color. The final decision was khaki. As the days progressed and the raids were heavier we were ordered into coveralls. This proved to be the only way to meet the existing conditions.

At the outbreak I was at Fort McKinley. A week after the first raids we evacuated intact and met the Fort Stotsenberg group at Sternberg; then we were split into smaller groups and sent to improvised hospitals in Manila. Most of the nurses by December 26th had gone to Corregidor or Bataan.

I was put in charge of a hospital ship on the 28th; I was to be given 10 nurses from the Philippine Red Cross to complete the nursing staff. Midnight of the 29th, the remaining Army Nurses in Manila left for Corregidor.

As you can imagine, the personal needs of the nurses in the Philippines becomes greater as the days pass. However, you will be pleased to learn that their needs will be attended to (if and when it is possible to arrange transport) through the American Womens Comfort Fund, now being organized by the American women in Australia.

The Red Cross ship sailed from Manila on December 31st. As the New Year was being ushered in, our Navy escort was leading us through the mined waters off Corregidor.

Our voyage down here was most eventful; all our problems had to be solved by improvisations. The greatest of the difficulties were, too many helpless passengers on so small a boat, a fire in the boiler room, rain, rough weather and plenty of sea sickness. At the present time, the patients we brought with us are being well cared for at an Australians Military Hospital. A week after the disposal of our patients, I was ordered as Chief Nurse to Headquarters, United States Forces in Australia. Preparations for the arrival of our nurses from the States began at once.

You can never know with what happiness and excitement I went out on the harbor boat to the meet the incoming convoy; it was like going home.

The Australian Army Debarkation Service and Nursing Group did everything they could to get our nurses settled here. The Australian Matron

The April 25, 1942, issue of The Army-Navy Journal *reprinted a letter I sent to my commanding officer, Colonel Julia O. Flikke, Superintendent of the Army Nurse Corps.*

in Chief and her assistants have truly been marvelous. One group of our nurses are on their way again; among them is Miss Newell. Before she left I had two long and nice talks with her. She was most kind; I had very many problems to settle and she was most helpful in spite of the fact that she was recuperating from the effects of a rough sea voyage. I was glad she was able to rest before taking off again.

The General Hospital unit are the remaining force. At the present time, the nurses of this unit have grand living quarters; very shortly, they expect to take over a hospital here in town—their work shall then begin in earnest. Among the nurses, there was but one uniform, a few capes and coats; our Quartermaster is having the rest of the uniforms tailored here and he is having considerable difficulty in doing so.

I thought you might like to know of a few things that would be ideal for the nurses to bring with them, articles that are impossible to purchase or rationed to the minimum: a foot locker (the present group luckily had them), and a large valise that could be carried, a flash-light, extra batteries and bulbs, shoes and hose, watches and alarm clocks, Kleenex, face cream and sanitary needs.

I shall keep you informed from time to time of the welfare of our nurses.

Very respectfully,

(Signed) Floramund Fellmeth

1st Lt., ANC

By early April, with the arrival of medical officers and enlisted men from the States and evacuees from the Philippines, Colonel Carroll constructed a medical staff that complied with the organization prescribed for medical corps in war zones, according to Armfield's report on WWII medical department organization and administration. By April 24, he had twenty-seven officers, including a colonel of the Dental Corps, a lieutenant colonel of the Veterinary Corps, and a captain of the Army Nurse Corps. Other sections, headed by a medical corps major, included hospitalization, supply and fiscal, personnel, evacuation, and sanitation and vital statistics.

Familiar faces

AT ONE POINT, I heard that a very dogmatic officer would be arriving to serve as the new quartermaster at our headquarters. We had difficulty in Australia finding a trained medical quartermaster. Then I was told to come to the general's office to meet the new quartermaster.

When I walked into the office, I recognized a face from my days at Fort Warren.

"Al Libasci, what are you doing here?"

We both hugged each other while everyone stood with their mouths open. I explained that before I left Cheyenne, I had been godmother to his baby.

As we spoke, I retrieved from my musette bag the bill of lading, which showed I had sent items home to Chicago. I wondered where they had gone.

"Well, I know where one of them went," he said. "Your things are all over the States. That ship had a near miss in Hawaii with the Japanese. It wasn't sunk but it was debilitated."

He said everything aboard was sent all over the United States. I gave him the bill and he said he'd track down my belongings.

More familiar faces reappeared in May 1942 with the arrival of eleven Army nurses evacuated from Corregidor on the USS Spearfish, a small submarine. The sub left Corregidor May 3, 1942, rescuing twenty-five Army and Navy personnel as well as two civilians. Ten of the eleven

When a new medical quartermaster arrived in Australia, I immediately recognized Captain Al Libasci from my days at Fort Warren, where I was godmother to his baby. Below, nurses Willa Hook, right, and Hortense McKay escaped from the Philippines in April 1942 and remained on duty in Australia. McKay took over for me after I returned to the States in the fall of 1944.

Army nurses decided to return to the States, but Hortense McKay wanted to continue working in Australia.

Only two other nurses who escaped from the Philippines remained on duty in Australia: Willa Hook and Ressa Jenkins, who escaped aboard a Navy PBY that left Corregidor April 29, 1942. The aircraft brought nearly two-dozen passengers to safety in Australia, including Lieutenant Florence MacDonald, who brought my 201 records with her. Ressa Jenkins asked Colonel Clement for permission to remain on duty in Australia to wait for her sister, Geneva Jenkins, who was on another PBY. That plane didn't make it out of the Philippines.

I met the nurses at the train station, where they had traveled across the country for seven days from Perth in West Australia. I wore the blue wool uniform, which Hortense described as "mighty attractive." According to McKay's biography, I warned the nurses against talking with reporters. I also described my harrowing journey aboard the Mactan.

For many months, Hortense and I lived high up in an apartment complex overlooking Sydney Harbor.

Summer of '42

IN THE ARMY HOSPITALS throughout Australia, doctors and nurses battled cases of malaria—a disease that plagued the medical corps throughout the war, especially during the last half of 1942 and the first half of 1943, according to Armfield's report.

Although rare in Australia, malaria brought by infected Allied troops spread throughout the continent, and by June 1942, half of the Australian forces in New Guinea had been infected. And Australian officials had previously bought quinine to treat the disease from the Netherlands East Indies, which fell to the Japanese in April.

The penetrating heat and intense humidity, along with frequent torrential rains, only exacerbated health problems among the troops and aided in the spread of diseases. In addition to malaria, the troops often fell ill with dengue fever and occasionally to deadly blackwater fever. Dysentery and tropical ulcers also posed problems, as did scrub typhus, ringworm, hookworm and yaws.

On July 10, 1942, I wrote a letter to Wally's parents, apologizing first for failing to write to them sooner.

"From the day of my arrival I've known no peace. I came to this place six o'clock one night and was at a desk eight

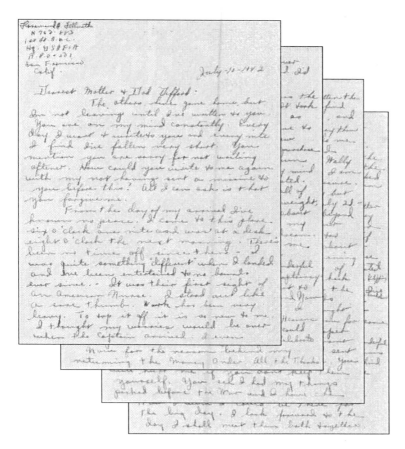

In July 1942, I wrote a letter full of news to the Diffords, Wally's parents and my future in-laws.

o'clock the next morning. There's been no time off since then. I was quite something 'different' when I landed and I've been entertained to no bounds ever since. It was their first sight of an American nurse. I stood out like a sore thumb. Work has been very heavy. To top it off it is so new to me. I thought my worries would be over when the Captain arrived. I even envisioned going home, but that is all over now. I am the assistant. I never dreamed I'd stay in this office.

"The hardest thing I found is the fact I'm alive and in Australia. It took so long to realize that people lived as they always did and that I would have to do the same. I arrived with very few pieces of clothing. I didn't want to

Seeing a need for more practical attire for nurses working in the field, those of us in Supply Services decided to create a uniform consisting of a culotte and shirt, so nurses appeared to be wearing skirts but could maneuver as if they wore trousers. I am in the center flanked by two other Army nurses.

purchase anything. There is no desire to own a thing. I was not morbid, but my mind was in the North, nothing else existed. It was so good and lucky that work took all of my time. I'm back to my normal weight, live in a lovely house (tell more about it at another time) and go about my duties as if I've been thru a bad dream."

I continued to thank Dad Difford for writing about Wally's promotion to captain. "I'm so thrilled and happy I'm about to burst the buttons of my jacket." I also asked Mother Difford to buy sheets and pillowcases to put away for Wally and me because I worried they might be difficult to procure later. I thanked them for the Christmas package containing a clip "too beautiful for words." Mother Difford also sent along a four-leaf clover and pictures of Wally.

"The linens I sent you from the islands please use. You will hurt me if you don't keep them yourself. You see I had my things packed before the War and I have the greatest hopes that they might have made the States on the last boat out."

I also complained about the inaccuracies in the newspaper articles about the Mactan's voyage.

"I am so very upset about all those paper write ups. They have exaggerated so. I've only had a small part of one (clipping). I don't want any more. I admit I've had the journey of my life but nothing as I've heard about. I wish I could go into detail, as I may not, my only and deepest hope is that some day I can tell you all about it."

In July 1942, the office headed by Colonel Carroll changed from the U.S. Army Forces in Australia to the Services of Supply headquarters, and Colonel Carroll and his staff transferred to the Melbourne headquarters of the new command, leaving behind the now defunct headquarters of the USAFIA.

At about the same time, after a tour of inspection of the forward areas, Lieutenant Colonel Clement saw a shortage of clothing and the need for a different type of uniform for the nurses in the field. We discussed what would be most practical and most economical, which is always a consideration. Finally, we decided nurses could wear a culotte and shirt, giving them the appearance of wearing skirts with the practicality of trousers, which is needed when bending over cots or climbing in and out of trucks. The uniform color varied from white to green after washing.

The culotte worked well, but the shirts proved troublesome because the tails would pull out of the culotte when nurses bent over a cot. They also were bulky around the hips and waist, which the nurses disliked. During another trip to New Guinea, Lieutenant Clement saw Australian nurses wearing what they called a Safari jacket—a shirt belted at the waist, cut fuller at the bottom and worn as a blouse. After discussing the idea with the nurses, we obtained permission to change the shirt to this design.

We also had to work with companies to obtain accessories

for the uniforms. With special permission—since shoes were strictly rationed in Australia—nurses could purchase from a company selling Selby shoes. We also worked with David Jones of Sydney to stock chamois color cotton gloves and other material.

At this time, through February 1943, Australia didn't have a U.S. Army headquarters with authority over all the forces in the country. Instead, they were divided among General MacArthur's Allied command headquarters in Brisbane and the Services of Supply (USASOS) where Colonel Carroll served as the highest-ranking surgeon in the theater, but without authority to issue medical directives to the Army's tactical ground and air force elements, Armfield writes in her report.

Throughout this time, the staff of the Services of Supply headquarters remained fairly constant at about thirty-five, despite the growing number of American troops in Australia, which increased from 105,295 in September 1942 to 664,508 by the end of July 1944.

In August 1942, the Army established an advance base in New Guinea, the first extension of the Services of Supply organization to that country, which later had seven bases and many sub-bases.

Still, the Army lacked any centralized and stable control of medical service, which left the responsibilities at the local levels and led to confusion from July 1942 through February 1943, when the Services of Supply changed to the U.S. Army Forces in the Far East. Then, in September 1943, it reverted to the Services of Supply headquarters. All of these changes "led to uncertainty as to the responsibilities and authority of Colonel Carroll and his staff," Armfield writes in her report.

As the Allies moved north in the Pacific Theater, the forward bases followed and built up while rear bases rolled up. The medical staff in the field faced tough terrain and a hot, humid climate. Usually fighting took place before establishment of any base, which meant hospital personnel often cleared sites of trees and brush and built their own hospitals and roads while caring for the sick and wounded, according to Armfield's report. No general hos-

Accepted. Nov. 12

The President,
Her Excellency, the Lady Gowrie,
the Chairman and Members
of the Central Council of the

Australian Red Cross Society

request the pleasure of the company of

Lieut. F. A. Sedensith

and friend

at the

28th Annual Meeting
of the Society
to be held at
the Town Hall, Sydney
on Friday, 27th November, 1942
at 8 p.m.

R.S.V.P. to Superintendent,
Australian Red Cross Society,
27 Jamieson Street, Sydney,
when an entrée card will be forwarded.   INFORMAL DRESS

I participated in social activities in Australia, including a Red Cross reception in November 1942. I am seen above in uniform on stage facing an audience with Eliot Palmer, Mrs. Stephanie Ormandy, Rear Admiral Russell Berkey and famous Hungarian-born U.S. orchestra conductor Eugene Ormandy.

pitals served New Guinea until after 1943, so patients were evacuated to hospitals in Australia.

Fall of 1942

AT THE END OF AUGUST 1942, the Services of Supply headquarters moved from Melbourne to Sydney because American troops were heading north. On September 1, 1942, we arrived in Sydney, where we stayed for a year. From Sydney, the Services of Supply oversaw bases in Australia and New Guinea.

As part of the administration, we made sure the nurses and nursing staff found adequate housing in areas close to the base, according to Maxine Russell's book *Jungle Angel: Bataan Remembered. The Story of Hortense E. McKay: A US Army Nurse Who Served in WWII in the Jungles of Luzon*. We also met the troop ships bringing other nurses to the Pacific Theater, orienting them to the city and identifying both work duties and recreational opportunities, such as movies and trips to the zoo to see koala bears, kangaroos, wallaby and wombats.

The surgeon's staff also made periodic inspections to the hospitals under its jurisdiction. During one such trip, McKay reported seeing Eleanor Roosevelt touring the hospital wards, her knitting bag in hand.

But Colonel Clement and I actually visited with Mrs. Roosevelt when she arrived in Australia. We sat with her in Colonel Clement's hotel room. At the time, Mrs. Roosevelt suffered from swollen feet after remaining seated so long during her flight from the United States.

McKay also spoke of greeting a unit of black nurses, under the direction of ANC chief nurse Birdie Brown. She said the black nurses, who had come to make a contribution, had to wait for their assignments.

The greatest danger for the troops came not from the enemy but from the tropical diseases, which often Army doctors couldn't diagnose because they were unfamiliar with scrub typhus and other fevers. Between October 1942 and April 1943, Armfield stated, fewer than 3 percent

I am seen at the far right on Christmas Day in Australia. From left are Polly Kirby, Mildred Dunmore, Cecil Gunn, Colonel Jane Clement, Colonel Frederick Petters and Captain Phil Weisbach.

of the men hospitalized suffered battle casualties, while 30.3 percent fell ill with malaria.

In part because of the confusion over who was in charge, the anti-malaria program suffered confusion during 1943 and didn't become centralized until late in the war, Armfield said. Starting in September 1942, General MacArthur's headquarters pushed for large-scale manufacture of anti-malaria supplies such as Atabrine to prevent the disease from defeating the Allied forces.

In December 1942, General Headquarters followed Colonel Carroll's recommendation in asking for malariologists and control and survey units to fight the disease. He suggested one malariologist, six assistants, three survey units and a dozen control units.

Colonel Carroll conducted inspection trips to New Guinea and recognized the need to help medical staff in New Guinea treat patients in the field rather than delaying treatment while the patients were carried back to the hospitals along the rugged trails. He developed mobile units—small portable surgical hospitals—that accompanied combat forces along the trails impassable to vehicles or mules. That way, the wounded could be treated immediately. He took staff from the hospitals and devised light equipment that could be carried in packs of forty to sixty pounds to treat the wounded in the jungles. He even created mobile laboratory and pharmacy units. By the end of 1942, he had developed twenty-seven of these portable hospitals.

"These portable hospitals saved the lives of many men who otherwise would have died along the trail on the way back to the field hospitals," Colonel Carroll later told an interviewer. His innovation earned him the Distinguished Service Medal, and he was later promoted to brigadier general.

From the time Colonel Carroll promoted me to first lieutenant that first year, I was never off duty—even on Christmas. I needed to learn so much about the nurses: their needs, their religions, their clothes.

We shifted from wools to cottons, and while some of the clothing arrived from the United States, most of it we acquired through a lend-lease program with Australia, McKay told Russell. It was difficult to find women the right clothing for tropical wear, she said, such as shoes, headgear, long-sleeved shirts, slacks and culottes.

Winter 1943

THE NEW GUINEA CAMPAIGN started in early 1943 and in February, the U.S. Army Forces in the Far East (USAFFE) was established with General MacArthur in command. Colonel Carroll became chief surgeon of the USAFFE and a few of his staff shifted with him.

The same month, three malaria survey units arrived in Brisbane and they reached New Guinea on March 22. General MacArthur's family physician, Colonel Howard F. Smith, became theater malariologist at the USAFFE, Armfield wrote. The program for malaria control started late in the Southwest Pacific area, after much damage had already been done to the troops in New Guinea.

We left Sydney on March 23, moving north to Brisbane to keep pace with the Army's advance in the Pacific Theater.

I had no choice when Colonel Carroll told me I needed to fly back to the States accompanying Doctor Herbert Vere Evatt, who was Australia's Attorney-General and Minister for External Affairs. The military wanted a woman along on the trip to keep Doc Evatt's wife, Mary Alice, company during the flight.

But when nurses were sent to New Guinea, the culotte uniform no longer served their needs because of the need to guard against malaria. The nurses needed to wear long-sleeved shirts, slacks and leggings so we had to create another uniform—this time slacks.

A prominent trip to the States

IN LATE MARCH 1943, I was asked to accompany a plane-load of prominent Australian officials to the United States. Dr. Herbert Vere Evatt and his wife, Mary Alice Evatt, planned to seek financial help for the war effort from the United States. Since Mrs. Evatt would be flying aboard the plane, officials decided another woman should accompany her on the trip, so they selected me.

I was headed for New Guinea and didn't have time to be away.

Colonel Carroll looked directly at me before speaking.

Above, from left, are General MacArthur's political advisor George Atcheson, Mrs. Mary Alice Evatt, Mrs. Jean MacArthur, Major Tony Storey (the general's pilot) and Colonel Laurence Bunker (aide). In the photo at right, Doctor Herbert V. Evatt, far left, is seen on an official visit to the SCAP, Supreme Commander Allied Powers.

—Both are US Signal Corps photos from October 1947, courtesy of the MacArthur Memorial in Norfolk, Australia.

"This is one time that you don't have an opportunity to say no," he said. "You're going."

On March 26, Captain Clement wrote me a personal letter outlining tasks for me to accomplish during a trip to Washington, D.C. In the letter, she said: "Miss you like a set of teeth already. Wish you would hurry up and leave so you could get back."

Doc Evatt, a man of small stature about fifty years old, served at the time of our trip as Attorney-General and Minister for External Affairs—in other words, as foreign minister of Australia. He had started in politics as an industrial lawyer and Labor Party member in the New South Wales Legislative Assembly, then served as the youngest-ever justice of the High Court of Australia, according to TheFreeDictionary.com by Farlex. He left the court in 1940 to return to politics, and when Labor assumed power under John Curtin in 1941, he obtained his position as foreign minister. (He later helped establish the United Nations and served as president of the U.N. General Assembly from 1948 to 1949, during which time he played an instrumental role in the creation of Israel.)

His wife, Mary Alice Sheffer Evatt, also known as "Mas" to her friends, loved the arts—modern or contemporary art in particular—and the couple bought many paintings from struggling young artists. She wrote poetry, painted and created sculptures, according to the Evatt Foundation publication, "A Fresh Point of View," published August 8, 2002, by Melissa Boyde. Although born in Ottumwa, Iowa, she lived in New Zealand before her family moved to Australia while she was still a toddler. She called her husband "Bert." She was in her mid-forties, and they had been married for twenty-three years when we took the trip to America. She and her husband had two adopted children, Peter and Rosalind. She also was the first woman appointed as a trustee of the Art Gallery of New South Wales, where she served from 1943 until 1970.

Also aboard the plane were a financial officer and the man who wrote the *New Guinea Diary*.

We left April 3 and made several stops en route to the United States. At one point when the plane took off, flames shot past our windows as exhaust from the motor ignited! Every time the plane stopped, it was parked in an isolated area and military officials immediately encircled it to provide security for the Australian leaders.

When we left the plane during a stop at Fiji, the Australians took me to the U.S. hospital, where I stood chatting with some of the people there. A telephone rang and I had a call: It came from one of the orderlies I'd known at Fort Warren in Cheyenne. He'd seen me and wanted to say hello. He now worked in the motor pool.

When he saw me, he asked: "Do you remember when you put me on KP?"

I said, "Oh!" I didn't remember, but I know he must have done something at the time to deserve kitchen duty.

At any rate, he felt quite proud speaking to me while his colleagues in the motor pool looked on.

The plane next stopped in Hawaii. I left the plane, wearing a tan dress I had designed, and we went to one of the American clubs. When we entered, one of our troops yelled to me: "Hey, Aussie!" He called me an Aussie! Well, the Aussies loved it.

On April 7 we arrived in California, where I called my family in Chicago to inform them we'd be arriving soon. We'd been told to keep the curtains closed, but as the plane landed in Chicago, I couldn't help pulling back the curtain to take a look. After all, it'd been three years since I'd been home. Later, my family told me they saw my face in the plane's window.

As the guards surrounded the isolated plane, I gathered all my belongings and prepared to leave. I needed help carrying all the things I'd brought with me, so the people on the plane each carried one of the items for me.

Police guards had escorted my mother and brothers Edmund and Bernard to a private room, where they waited for six hours for my arrival. I came in with arms full, but immediately embraced my mother. The finance officer cradled my music box while the man from New Guinea carried the spears I'd brought home for Captain

While serving in Australia, I continued to receive promotions. After Colonel Carroll promoted me to first lieutenant, Colonel Clement promoted me in May 1943 to assistant superintendent, captain, and in June 1944, I was promoted to assistant superintendent, major ANC.

Clement's nephew. Even the foreign minister, Doc Evatt, brought some of my items off the plane.

So I said to them, I want you to meet my mother. I introduced them all around. Then I bid the Australians farewell. As we prepared to leave the room, I turned to my mother and said: "Oh, by the way, Mr. Evatt's the Australian foreign minister."

"He's—what?" she asked.

I'd already gained notoriety among my family members for a lack of pretense and perhaps ignorance when it came to recognizing the importance of officials. My sister Colette later in life dubbed me "Miss Unconscious" because of this particular trait of mine.

The press also noted my homecoming with articles in the newspaper. One headline read: "Nurse Defies Jap Bombs, Visits Home Here, Weeps." The first sentence read: "An Army nurse, known for her iron nerve and resourcefulness

As part of my duties, I accompanied Colonel Clement on inspection tours in New Guinea. Above, I am seated in the center of the front row with medical personnel in New Guinea. At left Colonel Clement and I pose in rainy weather. Below, Colonel Clement, center, visits with medical personnel at Darwin in Australia. I am at the far left in the photo.

in the face of heavy Jap bombing raids, wept on her mother's shoulders this afternoon as she came home on a short leave for the first time in three years." The article also made reference to "an Army flier" in my postwar plans, but I declined to say when we would marry.

I flew from Chicago to Washington, D.C., to fulfill my assigned duties at the Army Nurse Corps headquarters. Then I took the train back to Chicago for a ten-day visit with my family, where Mother and my brother Edmund and sister Colette greeted me at the station. I asked about my dad, "the Skipper," who was waiting at home.

Another headline stated: "Chicago Heroine of Bataan Home." But that news story erroneously reported that the Mactan had been bombed nine times en route to Australia.

After the Easter visit with my family, I then flew back to Australia. A short while later a package arrived on my desk. I opened it to find a thesaurus, along with a note from Doc Evatt. I happened to mention to him on the plane that I didn't have a thesaurus, and he didn't think I should be without one, so he told an aide to send me his.

Spring 1943

After returning from the States, I resumed my duties as assistant director to the chief nurse of the USAFFE. Malaria still proved a raging problem among the troops, but finally, in April 1943, a malaria school was organized in Brisbane for medical officers and staff. The course consisted of lectures, practical field exercises and control work at an Army camp, according to Armfield's report. Nearly a thousand officers, as well as many nurses and enlisted men, received training at the school before the Army discontinued it in July 1944.

On May 15, 1943, I received a temporary promotion from Chief Nurse, a first lieutenant, to Assistant Superintendent, Captain ANC. Lieutenant Colonel M. Jane Clement signed the paperwork.

On June 13, I arrived in Brisbane, having traveled aboard

An article in the Australian Women's Weekly documents the contributions of Army nurses in New Guinea.

the SS Clip Fontaine. Five days later I left Brisbane for Sydney.

By the end of July, the Services of Supply had two 1,000-bed general hospitals and two 500-bed hospitals in Australia, as well as twenty-six station hospitals in Australian base sections and in New Guinea, each capable of treating between fifty and 500 men.

In September 1943, the medical section of the U.S. Army Forces in the Far East were returned to Services of Supply and Colonel Carroll, once more chief surgeon of USASOS, still headed the top medical office in the Southwest Pacific. Shortly before this change took place, the Services of Supply headquarters moved once again, this time from Sydney to Brisbane. So I left Sydney August 30, 1943, and arrived in Brisbane September 1.

Colonel Carroll still struggled with finding qualified men to fill key positions in the medical department, and he complained that the lack of a centralized organization added to the problems of issuing medical directives and having them carried out. The malariologists also transferred with Colonel Carroll, who pointed out that responsibility for malaria control now rested in three different independent commands. He emphasized the need for uniformity in discipline and education with regard to combating and treating malaria. In November, headquarters of the USAFFE finally issued a statement giving authority over malaria control to the Services of Supply, Armfield wrote.

I remained in Brisbane until February 7, 1944, when I returned to Sydney to work under Lieutenant Colonel W.R. Ridelhooper in the Quartermaster Corps. Four months later, on June 1, I received yet another temporary promotion—this time from Assistant Superintendent, Captain, to Assistant Superintendent, Major ANC.

I remember once in Brisbane walking out of a hospital and a young soldier poked another with his elbow while looking at me and whispered: "Is that a leaf?" He was referring to my insignia indicating my rank of major. The other fellow responded: "Yes, by damn, it's gold!"

First invasion night

I'M NOT SURE WHY they asked me to sit with Mrs. Jean MacArthur on invasion nights, perhaps because I had been sworn into the intelligence service on Corregidor. But the first time I received a call, I believe the general had led Allied forces into Hollandia.

The telephone in my room rang and I heard a voice on the other end. "Miss Fellmeth?"

"Yes," I answered, still groggy from sleep.

An official from the general's staff arrived at my doorstep and escorted me to the room where Mrs. MacArthur awaited news about the invasion and the safety of the troops—and especially her husband.

The first major Allied offensive took place in August 1942, when U.S. Marines invaded Tulagi and Guadalcanal in the Solomon Islands. The Allied forces proved victorious on Guadalcanal in February 1943.

In late December 1943—December 26—the Allies launched a full assault on the Solomon Islands and New Britain.

While I sat chatting with Mrs. MacArthur, who was in her mid-forties at the time, generals and other military officials gathered in another room to follow the invasion over the radio as it took place on the ground. I could hear them saying General MacArthur always insisted on following the plan that would result in the least loss of life.

During a lighter moment, we later heard that one of the staff from headquarters had given his dentures to a dentist at the headquarters office for repairs, but ended up called to the invasion before he could reclaim them. So he asked if he could have the teeth brought to him at the invasion site. Apparently, so the story goes, when they arrived on the beach he spied this young dentist so he crawled over the sand toward him and asked: "Where are my teeth?" But no one had told the dentist about the teeth. He didn't have a clue, other than thinking that perhaps this balmy captain had lost his mind. Here they were dodging bullets on the beach and he wanted to know where he could find his teeth!

I stayed with Mrs. Jean MacArthur and her son,
Arthur, and his Chinese nanny, or amah, Loh Cheu,
while General MacArthur planned and participated in
Allied invasions. This US Army Signal Corps photo,
courtesy of the MacArthur Memorial in Norfolk,
Australia, was taken in March 1942, on the day of
their arrival in Melbourne after they escaped from the
Philippines.

—U.S. Army Signal Corps photo.

Although I heard General MacArthur in nearby rooms at times, I never spoke to him personally. But I did develop an acquaintance with his wife, Jean Marie Faircloth MacArthur, a native of Tennessee. While we chatted through the long anxious night, she would often call to her son, who was about six, in her delicate and charming Southern drawl—"Aaaahh—rrr—thur." I'd look at the small-stature boy and he'd peek at me, then dash back behind a door or piece of furniture. His amah, or Chinese nanny, was never far from him.

Jean MacArthur and the general met in 1935 when she was traveling alone in Asia, and she proved a solace to her husband upon the death of his mother, Pinky, according to historian Carol Petillo. They married in April 1937 and lived in the Philippine Islands. In 1938, when her husband was fifty-eight, she gave birth in Manila to their son, Arthur MacArthur IV, named for his paternal grandfather, a decorated Civil War hero. As American defeat loomed in the Philippines, President Roosevelt ordered General MacArthur to Australia. His wife accompanied him on a PT boat when he left the islands in March 1942, vowing to return.

She always referred to her husband as "The General" or "Sir Boss," Petillo said. She was devoted to her husband, who towered over her physically.

During the nights, she often asked me about my family. Then she'd interrupt the conversation to chastise her son: "Aaaahh—rrr—thur." I stayed until the call came in that they had landed and the general had walked on the sand and everything was fine. So then I could go back downstairs. This happened a couple of times.

Mrs. MacArthur died in January 2000 in New York at the age of 101. Shortly before his death in 1964, her husband described her as "my constant friend, sweetheart and devoted supporter." In 1988, President Reagan awarded Mrs. MacArthur the Presidential Medal of Freedom the nation's highest civilian award, and called her "a shining example, a woman of substance and character, a loyal wife and mother, and like her general, a patriot," according to an Associated Press article about her death.

Joe E. Brown Hardly Closed Mouth All Day

Joe E. Brown scarcely had a chance to keep his celebrated mouth closed yesterday.

He spoke at a mid-day Town Hall Liberty Loan Rally, entertained American servicemen for 40 minutes in the afternoon, and made a brief radio appearance last night.

He spent the rest of the day rushing around Sydney by car, making plans for coming appearances, signing photographs, posing for pictures, and shaking hands.

Police, U.S. Army officers, and attendants had to escort him through a crush of autograph hunters as he left the Town Hall.

American servicemen carried him shoulder high from the stage after his afternoon appearance.

In the crowd outside the Town Hall Brown spotted an old friend, Chief U.S. Navy Photographer Homer van Pelt, whom he had not seen for two years.

Van Pelt was a cameraman on many of Brown's big film successes.

Rushed In Corridors

Hundreds of an audience of 3000 tried to head Brown off in Town Hall corridors after he made his Liberty Loan speech.

Brown said: "Australians have their own troubles and I'm not going to presume to tell you how to invest your money.

"But to be a real patriot today you must be 100 per cent, and not just give until it hurts.

"You must give with the feeling you are not hurting yourself, but going all out and enjoying it."

Brown yesterday renamed Lieutenant Erwin F. Virgin, U.S. Air Transport Command, who has been with him since he left the United States in January.

He introduced him to Lord Mayor Bartley as "Lieutenant Angel."

At the afternoon performance "Lieutenant Angel" introduced Brown as "America's only five-star general in the Pacific, alias Alibi Ike, or Elmer the Great."

A U.S. Army brigadier-general greeted Brown outside the camp.

Brown's audience, including Americans wounded in New Guinea who had been brought from hospitals, either laughed or applauded most of the time he was on stage.

"Gander At Kisser"

Brown started by saying: "I'm here to give you a gander at my kisser and to check on Wendell Willkie's expense account.

"My, say, the mainland (U.S.) has changed," he went on.

"Now a recruit is tested by two doctors looking into his ears.

"If they can't see each other, he passes. If they can, they make him an MP.

"I mean a military policeman, not a member of Parliament.

"Anyway, I don't care whom I insult —I'm only a civilian."

WORKS FOR PLEASURE

JOE E. BROWN, American film comedian, entertaining U.S. servicemen yesterday at a camp in New South Wales.

I briefly met comedian Joe E. Brown when he performed for troops in Australia March 25, 1943, but it was long enough to have a photo taken with him. I am second from the left. We met again in Spokane in 1963, when he once again insisted on signing the photo on the front.

Joe Brown entertains the troops

ONE OF THE HIGHLIGHTS OF 1944 proved to be a visit by wide-mouthed comedian Joe E. Brown, an actor who entertained American servicemen in Sydney, posing for photos, speaking to groups and shaking the hands of military men and women.

I had my photo taken with him and he autographed it twice for me—once in Australia and again in the States when he visited Spokane in 1963.

Brown, who grew up poor in Toledo, Ohio, started as an acrobatic circus performer in 1902 at age ten, then performed clean comedy in burlesque shows before breaking into movies in 1928 with a role in *The Circus Kid*. He published his autobiography, *Laughter is a Wonderful Thing*, in 1956.

He also acted in the 1929 movie *Sally*; *Hold Everything*, *Maybe It's Love*, and *Top Speed*, all in 1930; *The Tenderfoot* in 1932 and *A Midsummer Night's Dream* in 1935. He also performed in *Fireman, Save My Child*, *Elmer the Great* in 1933 and *Alibi Ike*, in 1935.

His son, Army Air Force Captain Don Evan Brown, died October 8, 1942, when his military plane crashed during a training flight in California. The following year, Brown announced his retirement from films. Instead, he focused on entertaining troops throughout the world.

He later returned to the cinema to perform in *The Tender Years* in 1947, *Show Boat* in 1951 and *Some Like It Hot* in 1959. He was eighty when he died July 6, 1973, in Los Angeles.

Returning Stateside

BY AUGUST 1944, the Southwest Pacific had eighteen malariologists, thirty-two survey and fifty-five control units—more than any other theater of operations.

In September, we established our new base in New Guinea, which the Allied forces controlled. It was at this

PROCUREMENT DIVISION
BASE SECTION
USASOS

APO 927
17 August, 1944.

Lieut. Colonel Charles A. Ritchie,
Quartermaster, Intersec, USASOS,
APO 503.

Dear Charlie,

       I am asking a little favor and I know that you will do
everything possible to assist in the matter. Major Florrmund A. Fellmeth,
N-702983 is assigned to (this office) the Distribution Division, as Army
Nurse Corps, Liaison Officer. As you know we were assigned to the Intermediate
Section as of 15 August, 1944. Major Fellmeth is very desirous of returning
to the United States under the present Rotation Plan.

       It had been planned that she would be returned to the States
on the September Army Nurse Corp overhead allotment. This allotment has now
been discontinued and Nurses on Overhead duty are to be included in the Rotation
allotment allocated to the organization to which the nurse is attached. Under
this new policy, Major Fellmeth will have to be included in Headquarters,
Distribution Division, Intermediate Section allotment.

       As for her eligibility for Rotation, Major Fellmeth left the
United States for the Philippines Islands on April 27, 1940. She remained in
the Philippines until her departure from there December 31, 1941 on the
Hospital Ship Mactan. She reported to the S.W.P.A. Command on February 6, 1942
and has been on duty with this department ever since, thus completing four years
and four months continuous overseas duty. She has been on duty in the Office
of the Director Army Nurse Corps until her present assignment with Distribution
Division, February 8, 1944.

       It may interest you to know that Major Fellmeth is one of the
most capable supply officers in the organization. She has been handling all
matters relating to woman's supplies and it has been a tough baby. I will
not like to see her go but she certainly deserves to be rotated if anyone does.
Furthermore it is quite a disappointment for this to come up when she has been
looking forward to returning in September.

       Please let me know whether there will be any chance of working
her in on the Quartermaster quota for the Intermediate Section.

       I am looking forward to seeing you, Bob and all some time
in September - wish I knew about when.

       Sincerely,

       W.R. RIDENHOUR,
       Lieut. Colonel, Q.M.C.,
       Assistant.

After more than four years overseas, I decided
the time had arrived to return to the United
States. My supervisor, Colonel Ridelhooper,
wrote a complimentary letter requesting my
release from duty in the Southwest Pacific.

time I realized I'd been on overseas duty four years and it was time to go home.

On October 3, 1944, I transferred to the Quartermaster Corps, Base B, in my position as a major.

After a year of being on duty every day, Colonel Ridelhooper of the Quartermaster Corps was forced to take leave and went into a hotel. Later he told us the stress became so great that he felt like jumping out of the window.

One day, I had been sitting for hours on a large rock on the airfield in New Guinea awaiting a plane that would take me back to Australia. Seated beside me was a Navy captain, so we started talking. He also had served a long time in the Southwest Pacific theater. He told me that the war in Europe was drawing to a close, and he figured the European staff would soon start to arrive in New Guinea and Australia, where they'd tell us how to operate.

I had been overseas for four-and-a-half years. Although I anticipated the return to the Philippine Islands, I realized that it was time for me to go home. I decided to ask for a transfer to the United States. It was granted.

Colonel Ridelhooper wrote a very complimentary letter asking for my release from duty in the Southwest Pacific so I could return to the States. He told me I needed to have something to occupy my time on board the ship during the journey home, so I went to a shop and selected a sweater pattern with knitting instructions. I had never knitted before.

On November 2, 1944, I sailed aboard the U.S. transport Sea Barb from Base B in New Guinea for the continental United States. The topside deck housed only four Army Nurse Corps lieutenants. Whenever possible, I sat on the deck and knitted. (When I finished the sweater and Wally tried it on, the sleeves proved to be much too long. He never wore it, but its purpose had been served.)

During my time in Australia, I had overseen all women's supplies, designed the uniforms, kept my pulse on all women's clothing—including shoes and underwear—and performed whatever duties I'd been assigned.

For my service aboard the Mactan and in Australia, I received the Legion of Merit medal. The citation, at left, states that the medal is given "for exceptionally meritorious conduct in the performance of outstanding services from 8 December 1941 to 27 September 1943."

Now I planned to return to the United States, rest in Florida for a while, then move back to Chicago and assume a post as a recruiter for Army nurses—after marrying Air Force Captain Wallace E. Difford Jr., whom I had known since 1936.

After I left, Hortense McKay assumed my duties with the Clothing Distribution Center Quartermaster at headquarters, British New Guinea, and working with women's tropical clothing. She had been stationed at Port Moresby, New Guinea, which was extremely hot, accompanying the women nurses as they stayed in the background, staged to move behind the troops through rugged terrain and sizzling heat.

In her book, she told author Maxine Russell that she traveled in November 1944 to Cape Sudest, accompanied on the plane by "two fuzzy-wuzzies," primitive New Guinea natives or "nature boys, wearing only the briefest of loin cloths and very colorful headbands." She reported having to carry high-topped women's shoes in sizes ranging from 5B to 11AAA, and she noted that the nurses nicknamed clumsy shoes "Daisy Mays."

In *Jungle Angel*, McKay described her typical day as starting at 6 A.M. and, after five hours, stopping at 11 A.M. for lunch and a "siesta" until 3 P.M., when work resumed until supper at 6 P.M., followed by additional work until 9 P.M., unless they attended a movie or church service.

Later, McKay worked at the 126th General Hospital at Hollandia, Dutch New Guinea, then boarded the Emily Weder Hospital Ship, which crossed the equator and headed for Leyte Gulf in the Philippines, where she tended to critically wounded patients at the 133rd General Hospital, a jungle hospital that grew to tend 3,300 soldiers. She said conditions at Leyte resembled those at Bataan except those at Leyte had better food, medical supplies and equipment as well as early triage, intravenous fluids and blood transfusions.

The hospital, which had only two concrete floors and the rest a muddy mess, began to specialize and McKay became more of an administrator. The hospital also had

When I left Australia, I took with me this "Souvenir of the Southern Cross."

Hortense McKay worried that she might break down upon the arrival of the nurses she worked with in the Philippines, who had been imprisoned by the Japanese for nearly four years. They arrived in a truck, happy to be free.

—U.S. Signal Corps photo

three wards of eighty beds each with Japanese prisoners, who were fenced in.

In February 1945, McKay learned that seventy-two women were coming to the hospital; they had been prisoners of war. She worried about breaking down under the stress and prepared her two assistants to take over if she seemed emotionally unable to hold up. She didn't know in what condition she'd find the nurses. But when they arrived, the nurses were sitting in trucks and waving, each one able to walk. McKay knew all of them. The women prisoners from Santo Tomas Internment Camp at Manila had nothing but the clothes on their backs, but the nursing staff at the hospital brought them nylons, nighties, soaps, lipsticks and other personal items. The former POWs were given physicals, intravenous vitamins and other medical care.

Chapter Eight

Life Back in the States
Marriage, Recruiting, Children and Reunions

I returned home to the
United States in the
fall of 1944 and married
Wallace E. Difford Jr.
February 2, 1945.
Newspaper headlines
about the wedding
described me as
a "Heroine of Manila."

Marrying an Air Force captain

SOON AFTER RETURNING HOME TO CHICAGO, I began planning my wedding to Wallace E. Difford Jr., a captain in the Army Air Force. We had to move up the wedding, though, because Wally had orders to report to India.

We were married February 2, 1945, at St. Augustine Catholic Church, the same church where I had been baptized, confirmed and graduated from eighth grade. Our reception took place at Edgewater Beach Hotel in Chicago. We were married in full dress uniforms since the war had not ended. We gave no thought to wearing civilian clothes.

Wally's mother arrived from Tacoma, Washington, along with her sister Gloria of Grosse Pointe, to join my family for the wedding. We had the wedding supper in the marine dining room of the hotel. Colonel Percy Carroll also attended the wedding, where we became Captain and Major Wallace Difford.

Wally, a native of Houston, Texas, lived in Louisville, Kentucky, before his family moved to Tacoma, where his father worked as managing director for the Douglas Fir Plywood Association.

Newspaper articles blared the news of our wedding, with headlines such as: "Nurse Heroine Weds Air Force Captain" and "Heroic Army Nurse Is Bride of Tacoman."

One of the newspaper articles also noted that the Mactan's exploits would be dramatized for the radio by National Broadcasting Company and aired over NBC chains. I planned to help in preparing the drama for radio and play a part in the "thrilling story of the rescue just in time to avoid capture by the Japs."

Forty-eight hours after our wedding, Wally had to leave for overseas duty.

As for me, I was assigned as assistant chief nurse of the 6th Service Command at Chicago, with the role of helping to recruit 18,000 Army nurses.

One of the best wedding gifts possible, however, was the

*For seven months in 1945, I shared my
story with radio listeners as actress
Helen Hayes and I read a script aimed
at recruiting more Army nurses.*

rescue of the sixty-four nurses I'd work with in the Philippines, when Allied forces recaptured Santo Tomas prison camp on Luzon.

Two weeks after our wedding, I received a wonderful letter in the mail from my dear friend Josie Nesbit, who referred to me as "Mrs. Wally" because she couldn't remember Wally's surname.

She also mentioned seeing Earleen Allen, who had shared a room with me at Fort McKinley, then mentioned the items I'd left behind in Manila when I boarded the Mactan.

"Your belongings in Manila are scattered," she wrote. "Meyer, O'Neill and others benefited by your clothes being brought into Santo Tomas by the Filipino nurses, a few at a time."

Recruiting with an actress

TO HELP RECRUIT MORE ARMY NURSES, I shared my story of life in the war zone of the Philippines and the trip aboard the Mactan. The Mutual Broadcasting System drafted scripts that we read over a microphone so the stories could be broadcast on the radio. After interviewing nurses, the radio people wrote a script.

Twice during the seven months I spent in the War Department's nurse recruiting drive, I performed the skits with stage and screen actress Helen Hayes, who had starred in such movies as *The Sin of Madelon Claudet*, *Arrowsmith*, *Farewell to Arms* and *What Every Woman Knows*. We performed together in Chicago and Minneapolis, and it was a tremendous experience.

The headline of an article by Edward J. Adamson about the actress's role in recruiting nurses states: "Helen Hayes Aids in Army Nurse Recruiting Drive; Actress stars on 'Voice of the Army.'" The actress had been referred to as "First Lady of the American Theater." She also received the American Legion Award for distinguished service to men in uniform on Armistice Day, November 11, 1942.

The script called for Miss Hayes to perform the part of nurse Floramund "Ann" Fellmeth, while I would ask her the questions.

But during the Chicago performance, the actress, who stood five-feet-one-inch tall, tended to speak too quickly in reading her lines. A prompter wrote on a chalkboard "Speak slower!" She told me she felt quite comfortable on the stage or before a movie camera, but felt daunted by the microphone. "The microphone bothers me," she said.

So instead, I answered the questions as Floramund—my own role—and Miss Hayes asked the questions. I spoke about huddling beneath the porch of our bungalow at Fort McKinley as the Japanese dropped bombs. On the radio, when I asked the Filipino soldiers and three other nurses if I should pray, I recited *The Lord's Prayer* too quickly. A man held up the chalkboard where I read: "Slow down the Lord's Prayer."

So I slowed it down—and he started shaking the chalkboard to indicate I needed to speak even slower—so I did. I'm sure that was the slowest rendition of *The Lord's Prayer* ever.

Reading the script, I noticed the role of Floramund, where I prayed the *"Our Father,"* indicated that I should end the prayer with these words: "For thine is the kingdom, and the power and the glory forever." But I had never heard that ending before, so when I reached the end of the prayer, instead I loudly sang in a Gregorian chant: "Aaaaaaaaaaa—men."

My mother and father, my sister and brothers and friends from church, priests, nuns and neighbors—probably sixty people in all—gathered around the radio at our house to listen. As I finished the prayer with the mighty Amen, my mother exclaimed: "Oh, she ended it correctly! Oh, my, wasn't that fine?"

The next day, Mother told me: "You were just as good as Helen Hayes."

Another relative who was riding on a train said he heard the radio in the bar and they announced a program featuring Helen Hayes and Floramund Fellmeth—and he told

Helen Hayes AIDS IN ARMY NURSE RECRUITING DRIVE. ACTRESS STARS ON "VOICE OF THE ARMY"

By EDWARD J. ADAMSON

HELEN HAYES on "Voice of the Army" program

TODAY the *Voice of the Army* presents with considerable pride the distinguished actress, Miss Helen Hayes in 'Names on the List,' a story of the U. S. Army Nurse Corps . . ."

Those were the announcer's opening words on a recent *Voice of the Army* program. And "considerable pride" was felt by all personnel, military and civilian, concerned with *Voice of the Army* productions. Here was an "All-American," "All-Star" show: Helen Hayes, who has been called the "First Lady of the American Theater," portraying one of our Army nurses, those angels of mercy whose sympathy, understanding, and skill have made them "All-American" "All-Stars" on our victory-winning team.

"Names on the List" was presented on the 808 radio stations broadcasting the *Voice of the Army* in conjunction with the War Department drive to recruit thousands of needed nurses. Miss Hayes, like so many others of her profession, contributes greatly with her talent to do all she possibly can to speed us on the road to victory. Her appearance on the *Voice of the Army* in behalf of the Army Nurse Corps recruiting drive marks an important signpost on that road. On Armistice Day, 1942, she received the American Legion Award for distinguished service to men in uniform and for furthering the war effort.

Miss Hayes can look back on a long career of personal successes in all fields of entertainment: stage, screen, and radio. In addition to her talent and delicate charm, her climb to fame was due in great part to thoroughness and hard work. She has been referred to as "prompt and reasonable and she outworks anyone around her." She is equally as good a listener as she is a talker. This aptitude stood her in good stead at the outset of her theatrical career. In 1914 she appeared in "The Prodigal," starring the great John Drew. The knowledge and experience the young actress gained from this greatest actor of his day were the real foundation of her dramatic career.

The year 1918 saw the young Miss Hayes rise to full theatrical stardom. On December 23 of that year she opened in the role of "Margaret" in Sir James Barrie's "Dear Brutus." Audiences and critics alike acclaimed her performance as great. Then followed a string of continuous successes, the most notable of these, to Miss Hayes personally, is probably "We Moderns," produced in 1924. One day after rehearsal of the play she attended a party, and for the first time met her future and now equally famous husband, Charles MacArthur, playright and newspaperman.

Miss Hayes' thoroughness is well proven by the fact that during rehearsals of "To the Ladies" (1922), the actress bought a grand piano in order to learn to play a Negro spiritual called for in the performance.

In 1928, while she was starring in "Coquette," which had a successful run of two years, Actress Hayes and Writer MacArthur were married. The marriage has been as successful as the careers of the husband and wife.

"Coquette" was followed by a series of highly successful ingenue parts for the actress, but in a revival of "What Every Woman Knows" Miss Hayes came of age in the part of "Maggie Wylie." In this performance Broadway discovered Helen Hayes, the character actress.

In 1933 Maxwell Anderson wrote "Mary of Scotland" especially for Miss Hayes and the play added, if possible, more luster to her star.

It was while resting at her home in Nyack, N. Y., that Miss Hayes first came upon the script of "Victoria Regina." She immediately cabled Gilbert Miller in London that she "must do it." In a few hours Miller's answer came back: "Everything all right, the play is yours." And it was her's, from opening to closing curtain. For a span of two and one-half hours, this slight actress (she's five feet one inch tall) from December 12, 1935, to January 1939, relived for thousands of Americans in hundreds of audiences from coast to coast the life, the times and the love of Britain's great Empress Victoria. Again, as with all her roles in the past, Miss Hayes tackled the part of Victoria with her usual untiring thoroughness. Before the play went into rehearsal, she made a rush trip to London to get authentic data from museums and galleries. In the play she became Victoria first, because she is a great actress, and second, because she took pains to get first-hand information on the Queen and her times.

On her twentieth anniversary as a full-fledged star, Miss Hayes played Viola in "Twelfth Night." After a performance, the late William Lyons Phelps came back stage to tell her he regretted "that the Bard can't be alive to see you."

Miss Hayes captured the acclaim of motion-picture and radio audiences with the same success she enjoys in the theater. Among the movies in which she starred are "The Sin of Madelon Claudet," "Arrowsmith," "Farewell to Arms," and "What Every Woman Knows." For her performance in "The Sin of Madelon Claudet" she received the coveted Motion Pictures Arts and Sciences Award.

Miss Hayes has been heard in numerous radio performances. On the CBS network she had her own "Helen Hayes Theater," in which she not only starred but supervised casting, production, and selection of material. Again, as in the other fields of entertainment, Miss Hayes was awarded the medium's highest prize. In 1940 she was named radio's best actress.

At the present Miss Hayes is starring on a road tour of "Harriet," which enjoyed a long New York run.

Helen Hayes has one particular ambition in life and that is "to go on acting as long as I can."

Page Three

An article about Miss Hayes appeared in the September 1944 issue of Army Life and United States Army Recruiting News.

others in the room: "Leave that on—that's my cousin!" So everyone in the bar of the train listened to the program.

Chief nurse at Gardiner General

AFTER RECRUITING FOR NURSES for seven months, I worked from August 1, 1945, until October 6, 1945, as assistant chief nurse at Mayo General Hospital in Galesburg, Illinois. At the time, some of the patients were German prisoners, so I administered the medications accompanied by a guard.

Then I accepted an assignment as chief nurse of Gardiner General Hospital, a 2,000-bed hospital in Chicago that treated primarily troops from Europe and family evacuees.

The hospital was dedicated to the memory of Second Lieutenant Ruth M. Gardiner, a flight nurse and the first Army nurse to be killed in a theater of operation during World War II. She died in a plane crash near Naknek, Alaska, July 27, 1943, during an air evacuation mission.

I thought I had been exposed to all the shocks of my life, but one morning I came on duty to find women sitting along the corridor walls, exhausted, with crying children and all sorts of baggage beside them. When I went to the office, I was told they were families of some of our military in Europe. They came by ship to New York and then by train to Chicago. They were on their way to California and we were a stopover.

"Do what you can," the colonel told me.

I sent four of the staff nurses out to consolidate our patients so we could move the families into the now vacant wards. I informed the kitchen to bring them food. Doctors checked each member of the families and did what they could for them.

We found it an extremely busy time but, believe it or not, we missed the families when they were gone.

One day, I received a call asking if we could take care of Helen Keller for the day. It seems she had made one presentation during the day in Chicago and planned to make

Not long after I finished recruiting, I took over as chief nurse at the 2,000-bed Gardiner General Hospital in Chicago. At left, I am seen standing in front of the hospital. Below, I am second from the right in the row of Gardiner nurses.

—Top photo was taken by the U.S. Army Signal Corps

another that night, but they wanted a place where she could relax outside of the limelight, so she wouldn't be pestered by reporters and bothered by the public. They were touring the world, raising money for the American Foundation for the Overseas Blind.

Helen Keller, who was born June 27, 1880, in northwest Alabama, suffered an illness with a high fever at nineteen months of age that left her both blind and deaf. She became a difficult child who tore apart the family home in fits of temper. When Helen was about six, her family hired a tutor, Anne Sullivan, who had lost most of her sight as a child, to teach their daughter, a deaf-blind mute. She began to teach Helen to spell words using her fingers, and it took a month before a breakthrough occurred when Anne spelled the word "water" while liquid flowed over Helen's hands from the water pump. From then on she learned to read and write, and became a lecturer and writer. She graduated from college, the first deaf-blind person to earn a bachelor of arts degree. When Anne lost her voice after a bronchitis bout, Polly Thomson started working as Helen's interpreter in public. Helen and her interpreters toured the world, raising money for blind people and helping to improve conditions in their lives. She championed the cause of blind and deaf people throughout her life. In 1964, President Lyndon Johnson awarded Helen Keller the Presidential Medal of Freedom, the nation's highest civilian award. She died June 1, 1968, at the age of eighty-eight.

I found a comfortable room near my office with a sofa and lamps where Helen Keller and her interpreter, Polly Thomson, could stay for the day.

I arranged for a meal to be delivered to the room and visited with her through her interpreter, Polly Thomson, for a while. I had to entertain her, but I couldn't stay the entire time because I needed to oversee nursing staff in the huge Army hospital.

From what I observed, though, Helen Keller was a very charming and incredibly smart woman. But she communicated through her interpreter, tapping out signals with her fingers into the hand of Polly Thomson, so her personality

I met Helen Keller and her companion, Polly Thomson, while serving as chief nurse at Gardiner. I am standing, fourth from the left. Below, Helen autographed this photo, writing: 'To Major Floramund Difford with cordial remembrances from us both Helen Keller.' Polly Thomson, on the left, also signed the photo.

came through Polly Thomson, who would state: "Helen says ..."

Helen smiled and she spoke, but in a bit of a gargled way. She autographed a photograph for me.

In my role as chief nurse, I helped close down Gardiner hospital, which wasn't needed after the war ended.

When Wally returned from India, I wanted to set up a home and raise a family. At that time, women couldn't remain in the service if they were married with children.

I resigned from active duty in the Army Nurse Corps on October 30, 1946, at the separation center at Fort Sheridan, Illinois. I had served sixty-five months as a second lieutenant operating room nurse and sixty-six months as a major in administrative nursing.

A summary of positions held states: Nurse administrative, nursing operating room; operating room supervisor and scrub nurse at Fort F.E. Warren, Fort Mills on Corregidor and Fort McKinley on Luzon in the Philippine Islands; assistant director, Southwest Pacific Area of Nursing Service in charge of women's supplies; and principal chief nurse, Gardiner General Hospital.

For what the citation described as my "heroic work" aboard the Mactan, I was awarded the Legion of Merit, established by Congress in July 1942 to honor members of the Armed Forces for "exceptionally outstanding conduct in the performance of meritorious service to the United States."

I also hold the following decorations:

■ Distinguished Unit Citation with two Oak Leaf Clusters

■ Theater ribbon with bronze stars for two campaigns— the Manila Campaign and the New Guinea campaign

■ American and Philippine Defense Ribbon with one bronze star

■ The Bronze Star Medal, awarded to the nurses in 1993.

I remained in the Army Nurse Corps Reserves and received a promotion December 1, 1947, to Lieutenant Colonel, ANC Reserves.

If I could only give you one lesson for life, I would teach you to love amidst all of the strife...

A poem by Wynona Bice-Stephens from her book, *The Art of Nursing*

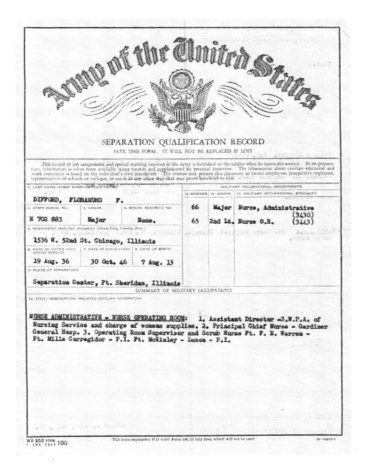

Army of the United States

SEPARATION QUALIFICATION RECORD

SAVE THIS FORM. IT WILL NOT BE REPLACED IF LOST

This record of job assignments and special training received in the Army is furnished to the soldier when he leaves the service. In its preparation, information is taken from available Army records and supplemented by personal interview. The information about civilian education and work experience is based on the individual's own statement. The veteran may present this document to former employers, prospective employers, representatives of schools or colleges, or use it in any other way that may prove beneficial to him.

				MILITARY OCCUPATIONAL ASSIGNMENTS
DIFFORD, FLORAMUND F.			66	Major Nurse, Administrative (3430)
N 702 863 Major None.			65	2nd Lt. Nurse O.R. (3443)
1536 W. 52nd St. Chicago, Illinois				
19 Aug. 36	30 Oct. 46	7 Aug. 13		
Separation Center, Ft. Sheridan, Illinois				

SUMMARY OF MILITARY OCCUPATIONS

NURSE ADMINISTRATIVE - NURSE OPERATING ROOM: 1. Assistant Director -J.W.P.A. of Nursing Service and charge of womans supplies. 2. Principal Chief Nurse - Gardiner General Hosp. 3. Operating Room Supervisor and Scrub Nurse Ft. F. E. Warren - Ft. Mills Corregidor - P.I. Ft. McKinley - Luzon - P.I.

I resigned from active service October 30, 1946, after more than ten years in the Army Nurse Corps. The medal at left is the Philippine Defense Ribbon and the one at right was awarded for the Liberation of the Philippines.

Wally's life before he married

BEFORE THE WAR, Wally had wanted to fly airplanes. He attended basic training at Randolph Field in Texas, but toward the end of the training, he developed astigmatism in one eye that prevented him from flying.

Instead, in 1942 and 1943, he served as Commandant of Cadets of the Basic Flying School at Gardner Field near San Diego, California, where newcomers to the military received flight training, ground school and military instruction.

He developed camaraderie with the cadets, who in their *Bee Tee* publication likened him to Abraham Lincoln. "Like Lincoln, this man may be best described as possessing a plainness that borders on greatness—sham and shallow vanity are unknown to him. In our dealings with him, he has proven himself to be both an excellent officer and a real friend. For his untiring efforts on our behalf, we take this opportunity to express our gratitude and best wishes for the future."

In 1943, when the graduating class dedicated the issue of the *Bee Tee* publication to him, it stated: "The Class of 43-E takes pleasure and honour in dedicating this issue of the Bee Tee to him. It is especially fitting to do so since he is leaving for greater responsibility in the service of his country."

He was then transferred to Fort Sumner, New Mexico, as Commandant of Cadets of the advanced training school. He stayed there for about a year and a half before being selected to attend Command and General Staff School at Fort Leavenworth, Kansas. After graduating, he returned to Fort Sumner where he became the base staff supply officer. Around 1944, Wally was transferred to Hobbs, New Mexico, as the Air Force supply officer.

Wally and I were married February 2, 1945, and forty-eight hours later he transferred to Greensboro, North Carolina, and then went to California to board a transport to India, where he served for fourteen months.

When he returned, Wally resigned from active duty and

DEDICATION

To CAPT. W. E. DIFFORD, JR.

From tents to 13 fine barracks; from ankle-deep dust to spacious lawns; from a few to many cadets; from a department of one or two officers to one of many officers; from a small area to the largest on the past; and from scattered training for prospective officers to systematic and intensive instruction, has grown the cadet detachment. All this growing-up was due mainly to Capt. Wallace E. Difford, Jr. The Class of 43-E takes pleasure and honour in dedicating this issue of the Bee Tee to him. It is especially fitting to do so since he is leaving for greater responsibility in the service of his country.

While I worked in the Philippines and Australia, Wally served as Commandant of Cadets of the Basic Flying School at Gardner Field near San Diego, California. He developed camaraderie with the cadets, who likened him to Abraham Lincoln. He then worked at Fort Sumner, New Mexico, and then at Fort Leavenworth, Kansas, then back to Sumner and then at Hobbs, New Mexico, before leaving for overseas duty in India.

CAPT. DIFFORD

Like Lincoln, this man may be best described as possessing a plainness that borders on greatness—sham and shallow vanity are unknown to him. In our dealings with him, he has proven himself to be both an excellent officer and a real friend. For his untiring efforts on our behalf, we take this opportunity to express our gratitude and best wishes for the future.

General Jonathan Mayhew Wainwright (second from the right in the photo) took command in the Philippines after General MacArthur was ordered to leave for Australia. After his release as a POW in 1945, he met with (from left) General Percy J. Carroll, me, Major Hortense McKay and Major Ruth Straub at Hines Hospital on the west side of Chicago. I rode back to the city sitting between both generals with a police escort.

worked with his father in the plywood industry.

After our marriage, we were living in Texas when I passed a kidney stone, just before I left the service, so they took me to Fort Sam Houston for tests to make certain I was fine. While a patient on the surgical ward, I'd heard about a very sharp colonel who put everyone on his or her best behavior. He had to make the rounds and check my test results before I could leave. Well, when he entered my room—why, I recognized him immediately from my life overseas. He said, "Annie, what are you doing here?" We gave each other a hug and he sent me down to X-ray. I was out of there the same day!

Although I loved my name, Floramund, I had to spell it to everyone so I went by my middle name, Ann, most of my life. If Colonel Carroll called me Annie, though, I knew I was in trouble or somebody was in trouble.

After Wally had resigned from the Air Force, military duty called again. He joined the Air National Guard in Spokane, Washington, where we lived for forty years and reared our three children as well as Japanese students.

Giving birth to four children

BEFORE HE LEFT FOR BURMA IN 1945, Wally and I had time to discuss children. I was the youngest of thirteen and Wally was the oldest of four, two boys and two girls. We agreed that if possible we would plan on that. Since I was born in 1913 and Wally in 1914, our ages and the school year came into our plans.

When Wally returned, I resigned from active duty, but joined the reserves and later became a lieutenant colonel. But I had to resign from the service when we had children.

Paula was born February 9, 1948, and Dana arrived January 7, 1950.

I then became pregnant with twin boys. Mark was born August 18, 1951, as a healthy baby boy. But during the delivery, Gary suffered injuries to his lungs that caused bleeding. They kept me awake and I could hear him crying. We asked a priest to perform the sacrament of the Last Rites before Gary died—only a few hours after his birth.

When I look at Mark, I can envision his identical twin, Gary Henry, who sings with the angels.

Later Paula filled the gap in our family when she married James "Jim" Gregory Renshaw September 27, 1975. He is our son by marriage.

A visit from Kathleen Norris

We HAD ANOTHER BRUSH with a famous celebrity while living in Redding, California, when Mark was just a baby. She signed the book we've always had near the door of our home where guests who visit can sign in.

Our guest was Kathleen Norris, an author from Palo Alto who wrote eighty-two novels that sold ten million copies, including her best-known *Mother*, published in 1911. She also wrote *The Heart of Rachael*; *The Treasure*; *The Story of Julia Page*; *Saturday's Child*; *Sisters*; *The Rich Mrs. Burgoyne*; *Poor, Dear Margaret Kirby and Other Stories*; *Martie The Unconquered*; *Harriet and the Piper*; and *Undertow*.

She had been in town raising money for the Republican Party. Republican leaders wanted to keep her isolated from the throngs, so they asked if she could stay with us awhile. I do not know why they asked me, other than they liked me and knew we could entertain properly.

I agreed, and they told me I'd have to host a group of ladies when they arrived with refreshments.

She came to our home March 21, 1952. I remember she breezed into the house and kissed Mark on the cheek. She wore indelible lipstick and after she left, I tried to wash it from his cheek. It took an awful long time to remove it from his cheek. She enjoyed holding Mark, though.

In our home, Wally has always done the cooking while I entertain the guests. It's very right that Wally knows how to handle the kitchen. When he proposed marriage to me, I asked him: "Can you cook?" I set a beautiful table and entertain many people quite well, but I don't cook. That's been my life.

Family life in Spokane

WE LIVED IN SPOKANE and Wally's parents lived on the coast, so we shared many holidays with them and five of their cousins. Every second or third year, I took the children by train to Chicago where we stayed five weeks. It gave them the opportunity to become acquainted with and enjoy my family. They visited all of the museums and enjoyed playing in a large attic filled with furniture, trunks of clothes and costumes.

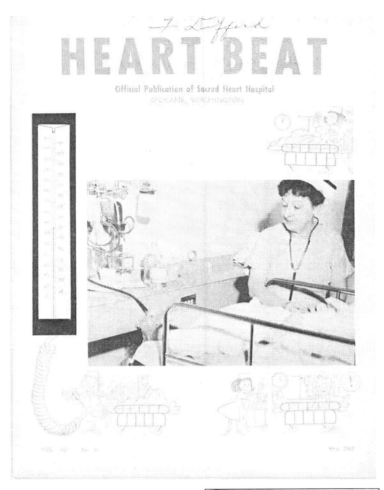

To help our children pay for college, I returned to work as a recovery room nurse at Sacred Heart Medical Center in Spokane. I retired in 1975 after working fourteen years. My photo appeared on the cover of the May 1967 issue of the hospital's magazine called "Heart Beat." I also donated my military uniform to the Fairchild Air Force museum in Spokane, Washington.

Our days at home included always eating in the dining room. We had never bought a home with an eating area in the kitchen. Dialogue each evening around the dinner table covered many subjects, including the fact that if they planned on higher education we would not remind them to study—that was their responsibility. I told them I would go to work to help with the college expense and did for over fourteen years in the post-anesthesia recovery room at Sacred Heart Medical Center in Spokane. I retired in September 1975.

Paula and Dana worked in the bakery at a local grocery store. Later Dana worked in the office at Sacred Heart. Mark worked a year as a paperboy and then in the operating rooms washing walls at Deaconess Hospital.

Our children also experienced many extracurricular activities. We were fortunate to be near an English riding school where they all learned to ride and performed at shows. The park nearby gave Red Cross swimming classes. Paula studied ballet and tap dancing for a few years and Dana learned Kabuki (Japanese) dancing and did well at it. All three children took piano lessons as well as figure skating lessons at the local coliseum. Mark wanted to golf and Grandpa Difford gave him his first clubs and six formal classes. He has continued this as a form of pleasure. Of course, all this kept them very busy but nicely involved.

Wally and Mark went fishing, which brought up the subject of a boat. We first bought a small boat, and four vessels later, we ended with a very large one, which we sold when we moved to Western Washington. Wally became Commodore of the Spokane Yacht Club and then Commodore of the Past Presidents "Blue Gavel."

After Wally's retirement from the military, he worked as an industrial appraiser and served as president of the appraisers society. He was also very active in the Spokane Lilac Festival and in 1962 became its president. Because of my background, we became very active in the German-American Club and were involved in all of its festivals.

While living in Spokane, I also entertained people at the Veterans Administration home, men who were isolated and not capable of functioning on their own. Three or four

THE UNITED STATES OF AMERICA

TO ALL WHO SHALL SEE THESE PRESENTS, GREETING: THIS IS TO CERTIFY THAT THE PRESIDENT
OF THE UNITED STATES OF AMERICA AUTHORIZED BY EXECUTIVE ORDER, 24 AUGUST 1962 HAS AWARDED

THE BRONZE STAR MEDAL

TO   MAJOR FLORAMUND F. DIFFORD, UNITED STATES ARMY

FOR   meritorious achievement during combat while serving in the
South West Pacific Theater of Operations from 7 December
1941 to 10 May 1942. The actions of Major Difford were in
keeping with the highest traditions of the military service
and reflect distinct credit upon him, his unit and the
United States Army.

GIVEN UNDER MY HAND IN THE CITY OF WASHINGTON
THIS   15th   DAY OF   June   19 84

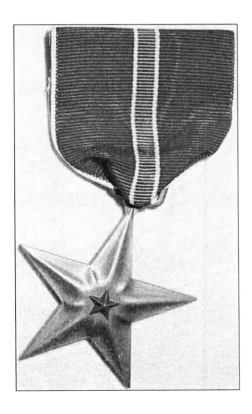

*In June 1984,
the nurses who served in
the Philippines received
the Bronze Star for
"meritorious achievement
during combat while
serving in the South West
Pacific Theater of
Operation from 7
December 1941 to 10
May 1942.
The seahorse figure
represents the
Philippines insignia.*

of us would visit them and bring lunches. They'd play music and we'd dance. I'd come home exhausted; I danced with all of them.

We also hosted eleven college students over a period of fifteen years—three of them from Japan. One of the Japanese students, Taeko, we've kind of adopted into our family. We exchange Christmas gifts every year, and we consider her children our grandchildren.

Paula was the first of our children to enter the military, a surprise because we had never brought up the subject. Paula said: "Didn't you know I would always go in the Army?" Dana first enlisted in the Coast Guard and then received her commission in the Air Force. Mark's forte was science where he first worked as a processing engineer at Masonite in California and then entered the Air Force, where he worked as an electrical engineer in Systems Command. While in the Army Paula met and married Jim, a regular Army officer. Paula changed to the reserve and graduated from the Army War College as a colonel. Paula and Jim are retired from the Army but continue to work with the Air Force and Army in a civilian capacity. Mark retired from the Air Force and is in research and development at Boeing. Dana continues as the executive officer of a reserve unit.

Years earlier when Mark was commissioned at Lackland Air Force Base in Texas, Paula and Dana had joined Wally and me for the big event. We mentioned that it would have been nice if Taeko could have been with us. This led to the start of the Taeko fund, where every month the six of us put aside an amount to be used for special events. This allowed us to celebrate several all expense paid gatherings, with the last one being a week's trip to Hawaii in February 2005 to celebrate our sixtieth anniversary in a lovely rented home on the beach. Our big surprise was Taeko and her husband Kanehiro joining us.

Reunions of the Defenders

IN THE YEARS AFTER THE WAR, I've given speeches at local schools about my experiences during World War II.

In May 1983, the Angels of Bataan and Corregidor returned to the Philippines for a dedication. Above, from left, are Ann Williams Clark (Australia), Hattie Brantley, Denny Williams, Rose Rieper Meier, Willa Hook Suess, me, Imogene Kennedy and Ann Bernatitus, then past the plaque are Eunice Young, Verna Hively, Grace Hallman Matassesin, Jeanne Whitlow, Dorothy Scholl Arnold and Ethel Thor Resper. In the center photo, I am seen on the right with Willa Hook. At right is a monument on the Islands to the American defenders.

I've been featured in newspaper articles, including one in the mid-1980s when I and other nurses who served in the Philippines received the Bronze Star.

After I left aboard the Mactan, most of the Army nurses tended the wounded in jungle hospitals on Bataan until they were ordered to Corregidor April 7, 1942. Two of the nurses suffered wounds in a bombing of Hospital No. 1. Other nurses worked in Malinta Tunnel on Corregidor,

Among eighty-five Army nurses in the Philippines, twenty-one escaped capture by the Japanese. Maude Davidson and Josie Nesbit selected the eleven who boarded a plane that left for Australia. Ten others—including one Navy nurse—escaped on a submarine. Another plane carrying ten nurses was grounded at Mindanao and those aboard became prisoners in September 1942.

Altogether, sixty-four of the Army nurses surrendered to the Japanese May 7, 1942, and spent four years in the Santo Tomas prison camp. Eleven Navy nurses who remained with the wounded in Manila also became prisoners of war when they were captured January 6, 1942, and they were later moved to Los Banos prison camp to establish a hospital. Two additional Army nurses, including Lieutenant Colonel Ruby G. Bradley, were interned in other camps.

Five Navy nurses also were captured and imprisoned on Guam.

Leona Lagstinger Stuphin took it upon herself to keep in touch with the nurses who served in the Philippines. When she died, I took over the role. I still send out a newsletter twice a year to the rest of the nurses—sorry to say only ten of us remain—and the families of those who have died. We produce a Christmas letter that lists all those who have died as well as the addresses of those still living. We enter the names of the deceased under a column called Parade Rest.

We've also traveled in our retirement years, including a trip to England and a return to the Philippines in 1983.

Wally and I have attended many national and Northwest reunions of the Defenders of Bataan and Corregidor. At

Above, Filipinos welcome the return of the Angels of Bataan to the Philippines. The 300-foot cross on Mount Samat, Bataan, commemorates the 35th anniversary of the liberation of American prisoners. Below, in May 1983, from left, are Army nurses Eunice Hatchett, Hortense McKay and Eunice Young as well as Navy nurse Ann Bernatitus.

Celebrating the 99th anniversary of the Army Nurse Corps at Madigan Army Hospital are Ethel Thor Nelson, author Beth Norman and me. At left, I am see cutting an anniversary cake. Below is the monument on Bataan dedicated to the Angels in May 2000. Unfortunately, my last name is misspelled on both of the monuments in the Philippines.

every reunion, I wear the angel bearing the Philippine insignia on one side and the two ribbons on the other. I had initially planned to wear my topaz jewelry from Sydney to the reunions, but the angel with the sea horse of the Philippines took its place.

During the reunions, I met a Navy nurse—Ann Bernatitus—who drew the short stick when one of the Navy nurses had to join the Army nurses at Sternberg. None of the Navy nurses wanted to leave her colleagues to work with the Army nurses, so they drew lots and Ann lost. So Ann ended up going to Bataan with a Navy surgeon. When a Navy submarine arrived, Ann—as a Navy nurse—was assured of one of the ten spots available for nurses. She therefore escaped imprisonment.

Lieutenant Ann Agnes Bernatitus was the first American recipient of the Legion of Merit. She received her award October 14, 1942, based on her service as a nurse during the campaign in the Manila-Bataan Peninsula from December 1941 to April 1942.

Ann is the only Navy nurse who regularly attended the reunions of the American Defenders of Bataan and Corregidor.

She joined us in 1983, when the nurses returned to the Philippines for the dedication of a monument on Mount Samat honoring the Angels of Bataan and Corregidor. Readers Digest published an article about the nurses' return to the Philippines.

In May 2000, at a reunion in Reno, Nevada, a rather nice looking gentleman addressed me.

"Pardon me, I understand you were the nurse on the Mactan," he said.

When I acknowledged that I was, he continued.

"I have always hoped to meet you. I am John Cook. I was one of eight Army soldier litter bearers to load patients on the Mactan."

We spoke a bit and he promised to send me a copy of an oral history interview he'd done. He had thought he'd be sailing on the Mactan as well, but they were left sitting on the dock at Manila. An old Filipino directed them to a lumber freighter that took them after dark the twenty miles to Bataan and Corregidor. The freighter crew abandoned the men, who dodged Japanese bombs and strafing fire, eating only salmon from an old can and a rind of cheese. In the wee hours of the night, as they were napping, they heard someone call: "Ahoy there, we've come to take you to Bataan," which they did. He became a prisoner.

Gardenia corsages

WE LIVED IN AN ADULT PARK in Spokane for thirteen years before moving west of the Cascades to a senior park in Tumwater, Washington.

In the Philippines, Mabuhay means "All that is good." We placed a sign on our first home that read: "Mabuhay" (pronounced Mabu-high).

One day while visiting our daughter Dana at Valdosta, Georgia, the sermon at Mass focused on the story of Elijah. He wanted to hear God and he heard him in the gentlest of winds. I touched Dana, who was sitting between Wally and me, and said: "Tell your dad we have a new name for our home." We had a sign carved and mounted on our house in Tumwater dubbing it "Whispering Winds."

I received a very special gardenia corsage for our fiftieth wedding anniversary, celebrated with our adult children in Las Vegas, Nevada, in February 1995. Upon entering our room, we saw a vase containing fifty yellow roses!

Growing in my bathroom I have a large gardenia, a gift from Wally, and a gardenia tree given to me by Dana. When it blooms, I cut a blossom and place it in a lovely small vase on my bedside table to remind me of all the special events in my life. The fragrance brings to mind pleasant thoughts and I am filled with gratitude for a life well lived.

All three of our children entered the military service. In this family photo, from left, are son-by-marriage James "Jim" G. Renshaw, Lt. Col., US Army (retired); Paula Difford Renshaw, Col., US Army (retired); Wallace E. Difford, Jr., Lieutenant Col., US Air Force (retired); Floramund F. Difford, Lieutenant Col., US Army Nurse WWII; Mark E. Difford, Maj., US Air Force (retired); and Dana G. Difford, Lieutenant Col., US Air Force Reserve. Below, Wally and I are seen in the 1990s at the dedication of a monument honoring General Jonathan Mayhew Wainwright in Walla Walla, Washington.

To celebrate their sixtieth wedding anniversary in February 2005, Wally and Floramund flew to Hawaii, where they spent a week with their children in a rented home on the beach. A surprise greeted them in Hawaii, where they were joined by Taeko, the Japanese woman they've informally adopted into their family, and her husband Kanehiro. Joining Wally and Floramund in Hawaii were their children, Mark and Dana, above, and their daughter Paula and her husband Jim Renshaw, below.

Bibliography
and
Appendixes

Bibliography

Adamson, Edward J. "Helen Hayes Aids in Nurse Recruiting Drive. Actress Stars on 'Voice of the Army.'" Army Life and United States Army Recruiting News, September 1944, Vol. XXVI No. 9.

Armfield, Blanche B., M.A. "Medical Department, United States Army in World War II, Organization and Administration in World War II," prepared under the direction of Lieutenant General Leonard D. Heaton, surgeon general, United States Army. 1963.

The Associated Press. Jan. 22, 2000. "Jean MacArthur, the Widow of GOA Douglas MacArthur, has joined him 1/22/2000." Found on the Internet at: http://www.nightscribe.com/Military/jean_macarthur.htm

"'Baby' of Chicago Family Is Lieutenant in Army: Nurse Promoted In Australia," Chicago Sun, Sunday, April 12, 1942.

"Bataan Anniversary on Red Cross Ship," The Chicago Daily News, April 1943.

Bee Tee, Army Air Force, Basic Flying School, Gardner Field, California. 1943.

Bee Tee, Army Air Force, Basic Flying School, Gardner Field, California. 1942.

Bice-Stephens, Wynona M. Major, U.S. Army Nurse Corps. *The Art of Nursing*. Dorrance Publishing Co., Inc., Pittsburgh, Pennsylvania. 1992.

Boyde, Melissa. "A Fresh Point of View," published Aug. 8, 2002, in an Evatt Foundation publication.

Bruce, David. Review of Joe E. Brown's autobiography *Laughter is a Wonderful Thing*. On the Internet at: http://oak.cats.ohiou.edu/~bruceb/Page5.html

Butcher, Fanny. "The Literary Spotlight," Chicago Sunday Tribune. March 25, 1945.

"Catholics Who Made the News in 1942," Chicago-

Herald, December 1942 or January 1943.

Cook, John. Oral history interview conducted by Katherine Clark on Nov. 14, 1997, with ex-POW John Cook.

EncycloComedia from Laughing Ferret Productions, Inc. Article on "Joe E. Brown July 28, 1892 - July 6, 1973" on the Internet at: http://www.comedystars.com /Bios/brown_joee.shtml

Fairfield, Major William A. Unpublished diary kept by the major covering the first week of December 1941 until the last week of January 1942. Given by the major to the author.

Feller, Caroly M., Lieutenant Colonel, AN, USAR, and Debora R. Cox, Major, AN, editors. Highlights in the History of the Army Nurse Corps on the Internet at http://www.army.mil/cmh-pg/books/anc-highlights/high-lights.htm and Highlights in the History of the Army Nurse Corps: Appendices, on the Internet at http://www.army.mil/cmh-pg/books/anc-highlights/append.htm U.S. Army Center of Military History, Washington, DC 2001.

Fellmeth, Floramund. "Nurse Writes From Australia," Army and Navy Journal, April 25, 1942.

Fernandes, Marian N. "Nurses' History," published in Camp Hill, Pa., area newspaper.

Foley, Norine. "Chicago Heroin Of Bataan Home: Lieut. Fellmeth, Now MacArthur Aid, on Easter Leave," Chicago Herald-American or Chicago Sun, Spring 1943.

"Former Belvidere Man Weds Nurse, Heroine of Manila," Feb. 10, 1945. Belvidere, Illiniois, newspaper. (*Editor's note: Headline is inaccurate as Wallace E. Difford Jr. never lived in Belvidere.*)

Foss, William O. "Last Ship From Manila," article published in the March 1984 issue of Sea Classics magazine, Vol. 17, No. 2.

TheFreeDictionary.com by Farlex. Web site address: http://encyclopedia.thefreedictionary.com/Doc%20Evatt

Goffredo, Theresa. "WWII Nurse Given Bronze Star," The Spokesman-Review. 1984.

"Hail Chicago War Heroine: MacArthur Hails Chicago Heroine," Chicago Herald American, Saturday April 11, 1942.

Hanson, Elizabeth. "U.S. Nurses Here Forswear Marriage For Duty," WOMAN, Melbourne, Australia. April 20, 1942.

"Harbor Defenses of Manila and Subic Bay," Office of the Harbor Defense Commander. Fort Mills, Philippine Islands. January 1939.

Heart Beat, the official publication of the Sacred Heart Hospital in Spokane, on the May 1967 issue.

"Heroic Army Nurse is Bride of Tacoman: Nurse Corps Major Helped Evacuate Wounded Soldiers on Last Boat Before Manila Fell to Japs," The Tacoma Sunday Ledger, Sunday News Tribune, Feb. 11, 1945.

The Army Nurse Corps: A Commemoration of World War II Service, on the Internet at http://www.army.mil/cmh-pg/books/wwii/72-14/72-14.HTM

"History of the Army Nurse Corps,"Office of Medical History, on the Internet at: http://history.amedd.army.mil/ANCWebsite/anchhome.html

"Joe E. Brown Hardly Closed Mouth All Day," New South Wales, Sydney, Australia, newspaper. March 1944.

Johnson, Bob. "Cook Relates War Experiences," The Recorder Herald, Salmon, Idaho. March 21, 2002.

Jopling, Lucy Wilson. *Warrior in White*. The Watercress Press, San Antonio. 1990.

Korson, George. *At His Side: The Story of the American Red Cross Overseas in World War II*, Coward-McCann, Inc., New York. 1945.

"The Life of Helen Keller," on the Royal National Institute of the Blind Web site on the Internet at: http://www.rnib.org.uk/xpedio/groups/public/documents/publicwebsite/public_keller.hcsp

MacDonald, Captain Florence, Army Nurse Corps. "Nursing the Sick and Wounded at Bataan and Corregidor." Presented at the American Hospital Association War Conference. St. Louis. 1942.

"Major Difford New Chief Nurse," Gardiner Pulse, Vol. II, No. 14, Oct. 15, 1945

Monahan, Evelyn M., Rosemary Neidel-Greenlee and Rosemary L. Neidel. *All This Hell: U.S. Nurses Imprisoned by the Japanese.* University Press of Kentucky, Lexington. 2000.

"Named to Gardiner Post: New Gardiner Nurse Boss," The Herald-American, Chicago. October 1945.

"New Chief Nurse at Gardiner Hospital: Southtown Nurse Appointed Gardiner Hospital Chief," Southtown Economist, Chicago, Oct. 14, 1945.

"News from the Rock: SOCIETY." Article on the Corregidor Players performance of the play Personal Appearance. The Stars and Stripes or Corregidor newspaper. 1939.

Norman, Elizabeth M. *We Band of Angels: The Untold Story of American Nurses Trapped on Bataan By the Japanese.* Pocket Books, a division of Simon & Schuster Inc., New York. 1999.

Noyer, William L. *Mactan: Ship of Destiny.* Rainbow Press, Fresno, California, 1979. Library of Congress, Catalog Card Number: 79-67032. Former chief librarian for the Veterans Administration Medical Center in Fresno, California.

"Nurse Comes Home From War: Nurse Defies Jap Bombs, Visits Home Here, Weeps," The Herald-American, Chicago. March 1943.

"Nurse Heroine Weds Air Force Captain," The Herald-American, Chicago. Feb. 4, 1945.

"Priest, Manila Hero, Promoted Captain by General MacArthur," probably in Buffalo, New York area newspaper.

The Quan, publication of the American Defenders of Bataan and Corregidor. "Floramund Fellmeth Difford," McKees Rocks, Pennsylvania. February 2004.

Rathe, Sgt. Chuck. "Last Ship Out of Manila: The aging USS Mactan dumped its cargo and became a mercy ship on New Year's Day 1942." YANK, The Army Weekly. World War II soldiers' magazine. Probably 1945.

"Red Cross Ship Evacuates Manila Wounded," The Red Cross Courier. May 1942. May 1942.

"Rites for Two of Gen. MacArthur's Forces," Makassar newspaper. January 1941.

Russell, Maxine K. *Jungle Angel: Bataan Remembered. The Story of Hortense E. McKay: A US Army Nurse Who Served in WWII in the Jungles of Luzon.* As told to Maxine K. Russell. The Military Historical Society of Minnesota. 1988.

Shanahan, Rev. T, S.J., "Jesuit from the Philippines Now in Melbourne," Date and newspaper unknown. Herald-American photo

The Spokesman-Review, Nov. 11, 1987.

Stromnes, John. "Women at War: Decorated WWII Vet Says There's No Turning Back," The Missoulian, June 17, 1991.

Telephone Directory, Manila and Vicinity, Directory of All Officers Stationed within the Philippine Department, Headquarters Philippine Department, Manila, P.I., July 16, 1941. Copied from Washington, D.C., archives.

"USA Nurses in Australia," Herald Feature Service. Melbourne, Australia.

Waldon, Kerrie. "A Dangerous Voyage." That's Life: Our Family Album, New South Wales. (Feature on Red Cross nurse Miriam Fowles.)

Wong, Ken. "Filipino MD recalls WWII fighting in his homeland," San Francisco Examiner, April 16, 1980.

Appendix I

Here is a list of U.S. Army nurses in the Philippines and what became of them after the war started—and later when they returned home to the States.

Army nurse who went to Australia on hospital ship Mactan from Manila at midnight, Dec. 31, 1941. After the twenty-seven day journey, she remained in Australia to set up the nursing service.

1. Floramund A. Fellmeth, Chicago, Illinois

Army nurses who left Corregidor by P.B.Y. April 29, 1942

1. Catherine M. Acorn

2. Dorothea M. Daley, Hamilton, Missouri

3. Susan Downing Gallagher

4. Eunice C. Hatchitt, Prairie Lea, Texas

5. Ressa Jenkins, Sevierville, Tennessee

6. Willa Hook, Renfrow, Oklahoma

7. Harriet G. Lee, Boston, Massachusetts

8. Mary G. Lohr, Greensburg, Pennsylvania

9. Florence MacDonald, Brockton, Massachusetts

10. Juanita Redmond, Swansea, South Carolina

Army nurses who left Corregidor by submarine May 3, 1942

1. Leona Gastinger, Alabama

2. Nancy J. Gillahan

3. Grace D. Hallman, Georgia

4. Hortense McKay, Amherst, Minnesota

5. Mary L. Moultrie, Georgia

6. Mollie A. Peterson, Arkansas

7. Ruth W. Straub, Milwaukee, Wisconsin

8. Helen Summers, Queens, New York

9. Lucy Wilson, Big Sandy, Texas

10. Beth A. Veley, San Jose, California

11. Mabel V. Stevens, Nebraska

Navy nurse who left Corregidor by submarine May 3, 1942

1. Ann Bernatitus, Exeter, Pennsylvania

Army nurses who were on a P.B.Y. that did not make it from Mindinao April 29, 1942, and became printers of war.

1. Earleen Allen, Chicago, Illinois

2. Louise M. Anschicks, Mendota, Illinois

3. Agnes D. Barre, Orange, Texas

4. Ethel L. Blaine, Bible Grove, Missouri

5. Helen L. Gardner, Aberdeen, Ohio

6. Rosemary Hogan, Chattanooga, Oklahoma

7. Geneva Jenkins, Sevierville, Tennessee

8. Eleanor O'Neill, Providence, Rhode Island

9. Rita G. Palmer, Hampton, New Hampshire

10. Evelyn B. Whitlow, Leasburg, North Carolina

Army Nurse Corps prisoners of war

1. Maude Campbell Davison, Washington, D.C.

2. Josephine May "Josie" Nesbit, Parlin, Colorado

3. Mina A. Aasen, Minot, North Dakota

4. Phyllis J. Arnold, Minneapolis, Minnesota

5. Clara Mae Bickford, Tivoli, Texas

6. Earlyn "Blackie" Black, Groesbeck, Texas

7. Ruby G. Bradley, Spencer, West Virginia

8. Hattie R. Brantley, Jefferson, Texas

9. Minnie L. Breese, Arlington Heights, Illinois

10. Myra V. Burris, San Antonio, Texas

11. Helen Cassiani, Bridgewater, Massachusetts

12. Beatrice E. Chambers, Manila, Philippine Islands

13. Edith M. Corns, Cleveland, Ohio

14. Mildred Dalton, Jefferson,

15. Georgia Kathyrn L. Dollason, Augusta, Georgia

16. Sallie P. Durrett, Louisville, Kentucky

17. Bertha Dworsky, Halletsville, Texas

18. Dorcas E. Easterling, Abbot, Texas

19. Magdalena Eckman, Pine Grove, California

20. Eula R. Fails, Houston, Texas

21. Adele F. Foreman, Masten, Pennsylvania

22. Eleanor Mae Garen, South Bend, Indiana

23. Marcia L. Gates, Janesville, Wisconsin

24. Beulah M. Greenwalt, Seattle, Washington

25. Alice J. Hahn, Chicago, Illinois

26. Helen M. Hennessey, Leavenworth, Kansas

27. Gwendolyn L. Henshaw, Los Angeles, California

28. Verna V. Henson, Trinity, Texas

29. Doris A. Kehoe, Pacific Grove, California

30. Imogene Kennedy, Philadelphia, Mississippi

31. Blanche Kimball, Topeka, Kansas

32. Eleanor O. Lee, Lonaconing, Maryland

33. Frankie T. Lewey, Dalhart, Texas

34. Dorothy L. Ludlow, Little Rock, Arkansas

35. Inez V. McDonald, Tupelo, Mississippi

36. Letha McHale, Haverhill, Massachusetts

37. Winifred P. Madden, Montello, Wisconsin

38. Gladys Ann Mealor, Gorgas, Alabama

39. Mary Brown Menzie, New Orleans, Louisiana

40. Adolpha M. Meyer, St. Louis, Missouri

41. Clara L. Mueller, Philadelphia, Pennsylvania

42. Frances Louise Nash, Washington, Georgia

43. Mary J. Oberst, Owensboro, Kentucky

44. Beulah M. Putnam, Worthington, Ohio

45. Mary J. Reppak, Shelton, Connecticut

46. Rose F. Rieper, St. Louis, Missouri

47. Dorothy Scholl, Independence, Missouri

48. Edith E. Shacklette, Brandenberg, Kentucky

49. Ruth M. Stoltz, Dayton, Ohio

50. Ethel M. Thor, Tacoma, Washington

51. Madeline M. Ullom, O'Neill, Nebraska

52. Anna E. Williams, Harrisburg, Pennsylvania

53. Edith M. Wimberly, Campti, Louisiana

54. Anne B. Wurts, Leominster, Massachusetts

55. Eunice F. Young, Arkport, New York

56. Alice M. "Swish" Zwicker, Brownville, Maine

Navy nurses who became prisoners of war

1. Chief Nurse Laura Mae Cobb, Wichita, Kansas

2. Mary F. Chapman, Chicago, Illinois

3. Bertha R. Evans, Portland, Oregon

4. Helen C. Gorzelanski, Omaha, Nebraska

5. Mary Rose Harrington, Elk Point, South Dakota

6. Margaret A. Nash, Wilkes-Barre, Pennsylvania

7. Goldia A. O'Haver, Hayfield, Minnesota

8. Eldene E. Paige, Lomita, California

9. Susie J. Pitcher, Des Moines, Iowa

10. Dorothy Still, Long Beach, California

11. Edwina Todd, Pomona, California

Nurses imprisoned with the Navy nurses

1. Helen G. Grant, Scottish nurse

2. Basilia Torres Steward, wife of an American

Appendix II

SQUADRON AND DISTINCTIVE INSIGNIA
(Lineages through 8 April 1942)

Hqs and Special Troops, Philippine Division. The division was organized on 8 June 1921. **Campaigns:** WW2: *Philippine Islands.*	**12th Quartermaster Regiment (PS):** Organized 1922 as Philippine Division Quartermaster Train. **Campaigns:** WW2: *Philippine Islands.*	**NO DI** — **192nd Tank Battalion (Wisc., Ill., Ohio, Ky. National Guard):** Constituted 1940 by redesignation of 32nd, 33rd, 37th, and 38th Tank Cos. Inducted into federal service 1940.
31st Infantry: Organized 1916. **Campaigns:** WW1: Siberia. WW2: *Philippine Islands.*	**12th Signal Company (PS):** Lineage unknown. **Campaigns:** WW2: *Philippine Islands.*	**2nd Observation Squadron:** Organized 1915. After various redesignations, redesignated 2nd Obsn Sqn 1924. **Campaigns:** WW2: *Philippine Islands.*
43rd Infantry (PS): Organized 1917. Consolidated 1920 with 2nd, 8th, and 13th Battalions, Philippine Scouts and redesignated 43rd Inf (PS). **Campaigns:** WW2: *Philippine Islands.* (Illustrated insignia is a post-war "E" class.)	**26th Cavalry Regiment (PS):** Organized 1922 by transfer of personnel from 25th FA (PS). **Campaigns:** WW2: *Philippine Islands.*	**NO DI** — **3rd Pursuit Squadron:** Organized 1917 as 3rd Aero Sqn. Redesignated 1924. **Campaigns:** WW2: *Philippine Islands.* (Aircraft insignia only.)
45th Infantry (PS): Organized 1918 as 1st Philippine Inf (Prov) from existing scout battalions. Consolidated with 45th Inf in 1920. **Campaigns:** *Philippine Insurrection:* Luzon 1900, 1901, 1902. WW2: *Philippine Islands.*	**59th Coast Artillery (Tractor Drawn manning Harbor Defense):** Organized 1918 from existing batteries. **Campaigns:** Civil War: Gettysburg; WW1: Lorraine, St. Mihiel, Meuse-Argonne; WW2: *Philippine Islands.*	**4th Composite Group:** Organized 1920 as 1st Observation Group. Redesignated 4th GP (obsn) 1921, 4th Gp (Comp) 1922. Inactivated 1941. **Campaigns:** WW1: Lorraine, St. Mihiel, Meuse-Argonne.
57th Infantry (PS): Organized 1918 from existing scout battalions as 2nd Philippine Infantry (Prov). Consolidated 1920 with 57th Infantry. **Campaigns:** *Philippine Insurrection:* Luzon 1901, 1902; WW2: *Philippine Islands.*	**60th Coast Artillery (Anti-Aircraft):** Organized 1922 from existing batteries as 60th CA Battalion. Expanded 1924. **Campaigns:** WW2: *Philippine Islands.*	**5th Air Base Group:** Lineage unavailable. **Campaigns:** Ww2: *Philippine Islands.*
NO DI — **23rd Field Artillery (PS):** Constituted inactive 1921. Activated 1936. **Campaigns:** WW2: *Philippine Islands.*	**91st Coast Artillery (Harbor Defense) (PS):** Organized 1924 from existing scout batteries. **Campaigns:** WW2: *Philippine Islands.*	**7th Bombardment Group (Heavy):** Organized 1919 as 1st Army Obsn Gp. Redesignated 7th Gp (Obsn) 1921. Inactivated 1921. Redesignated 7th Bomb Gp 1923 and activated 1928. **Campaigns:** WW1: Lorraine, St. Mihiel, Meuse-Argonne; WW2: *Philippine Islands* (elements, ground echelon); East Indies.
24th Field Artillery (PS): Organized 1918 as 1st Philippine Artillery (Prov) from existing scout battalions. Redesignated 1921. **Campaigns:** *Philippine Insurrection:* Mindanao; WW2: *Philippine Islands.*	**92nd Coast Artillery (Harbor Defense manning Tractor Drawn) (PS):** Organized 1924 from existing scout batteries. **Campaigns:** WW2: *Philippine Islands.*	**NO DI** — **20th Pursuit Squadron:** Constituted 1939 and activated 1940. **Campaigns:** WW2: *Philippine Islands.*
NO DI — **86th Field Artillery (PS):** Constituted inactive 1927. Activated 1941. **Campaigns:** WW2: *Philippine Islands.*	**200th Coast Artillery (Anti-Aircraft) (New Mexico National Guard):** Organized 1883 as 1st New Mexico Cavalry. After various redesignations, redesignated 111th Cavalry in 1922. Redesignated CAC, later 200th CAC in 1940. Inducted into federal service 1941. **Campaigns:** Indian Wars: Apaches; War with Spain: Santiago; WW1: without inscription; WW2: *Philippine Islands.*	**19th Bombardment Group (Heavy):** Constituted 1927 as 19th Obsn Gp. Redesignated 19th Bomb Gp 1929 and activated 1932. **Campaigns:** WW2: *Philippine Islands, East Indies.*
NO DI — **88th Field Artillery (PS):** Constituted inactive 1933. Activated 1941. **Campaigns:** WW2: *Philippine Islands.*		**20th Air Base Group:** Lineage unavailable. **Campaigns:** WW2: *Philippine Islands.*
14th Engineers (PS): Organized 1918 as 1st Philippine Engineers (Prov) from existing battalions. Redesignated 1921. **Campaigns:** WW2: *Philippine Islands.*	**NO DI** — **515th Coast Artillery (Anti-Aircraft):** Organized 1941 by expansion and redesignation of one battalion 200th CAC (AA). **Campaigns:** WW2: *Philippine Islands.*	**17th Pursuit Squadron:** Organized 1917 and redesignated 17th Aero Sqn. Redesignated 17th Pursuit Sqn 1936. **Campaigns:** WW1: Picardy, Somme Defensive, Flanders, Somme Offensive, Lorraine, Champagne, Champagne-Marne, Aisne-Marne, St. Mihiel, Meuse-Argonne; WW2: *Philippine Islands.*
12th Medical Regiment (PS): Organized 1922. **Campaigns:** WW2: *Philippine Islands.*	**194th Tank Battalion (Min, Mo, Cal, National Guard):** Constituted 1940 by redesignation of 34th, 35th, and 40th Tank Cos. Inducted into federal service 1940. **Campaigns:** WW2: *Philippine Islands.* (DI approved 1952.)	**NO DI** — **24th Pursuit Group:** Organized 1941. **Campaigns:** WW2: *Philippine Islands.*

NO DI	**30th Bombardment Squadron:** Organized 1921 as 30th Aero Sqn. Redesignated 30th Bomb Sqn 1932. Aircraft insignia adopted in 1953. **Campaigns:** WW1: without inscription; WW2: Philippine Islands.	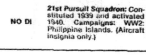	**1st Chemical Company:** Organized 1917 as Co. C, 30th Engineers. Redesignated Co. C, 1st Gas Regiment 1918, 1st Chemical Co. 1927. **Campaigns:** WW2: Philippine Islands (1st Platoon only)
NO DI	**93rd Bombardment Squadron:** Organized 1917 as 93rd Aero Sqn. After various redesignations, redesignated 93rd Bomb Sqn 1936. **Campaigns:** WW1: Lorraine, St. Mihiel, Meuse-Argonne; WW2: Philippine Islands, East Indies. (Aircraft insignia only.)	NO DI	**21st Pursuit Squadron:** Constituted 1939 and activated 1940. **Campaigns:** WW2: Philippine Islands. (Aircraft insignia only.)

	803rd Engineer Aviation Battalion: Organized 1941. **Campaigns:** WW2: Philippine Islands. (DI adopted in postwar period.)	NO DI	**34th Pursuit Squadron:** Constituted 1939 and activated 1940. **Campaigns:** WW2: Philippine Islands.
	Harbor Defenses of Manila and Subic Bays: Lineage unavailable. **Campaigns:** WW2: Philippine Islands. (Illustration is one of the coat of arms of the unit. No DI was approved.)		**14th Bombardment Squadron:** Organized 1917 as 14th Aero Sqn. Consolidated with Bolling Field Detachment 1935 as 14th Bomb Sqn and inactivated 1935. Activated 1940. **Campaigns:** WW2: Philippine Islands, East Indies.

	28th Bombardment Squadron: Organized 1917 as 28th Aero Sqn. After various redesignations, redesignated 28th Bomb Sqn 1922. **Campaigns:** WW1: Flanders, Lys, Lorraine, St. Mihiel, Meuse-Argonne; WW2: Philippine Islands.
	27th Bombardment Group (Light): Constituted 1939 and activated 1940. **Campaigns:** WW2: Philippine Islands, East Indies.
	35th Pursuit Group: Constituted 1939. Activated 1940. **Campaigns:** Philippine Islands (21st and 34th Pursuit Squadrons only); East Indies.

In September 1982, The Quan published a list showing the squadron and distinctive insignias for military service during World War II through April 8, 1942. Reprinted here with permission of The Quan.